PREFACE.

HISTORY enriches the mind, gratifies a worthy desire to be informed on past events, enables us to avail ourselves of the experience of our predecessors, informs and regulates our judgment, and is profitable for reproof and correction.

The earliest records of humanity are found in the Sacred Scripture, and for that reason have a strong claim on our diligent study. Next to inspired history, our own town, our own county, our own State, our own common country and the deeds of our fore-fathers who first settled and improved the land or country we call our own, should receive our notice. To Americans, a knowledge of American history is essential.

A second and third generation are now enjoying the fruits that resulted from toils and perils of their industrious and frugal ancestors, and what a contrast between circumstances and appearances *then* and *now!* The tangled forest is gone, the beasts of prey that prowled are gone, the war-whoop of the red man is hushed, the wigwams are wasted away by the rot of time, and the council-fires are long since extinguished, and in their stead we have fertile fields, smiling gardens, commodious dwellings, well arranged school-houses, civilized communities, edifices erected and dedicated to the worship of God. Time, culture and science have wrought a transformation.

PREFACE.

It is my design to give a comprehensive history of those who followed the devious Indian foot-path through the wilderness of this part of the Western Reserve and established themselves in what is now called Medina county, and in my narratives I must necessarily observe brevity. Many important incidents must remain untold because those who took part in them died before their deeds were recorded.

All that I have compiled was gathered either from manuscripts or from the oral statements of those who saw or knew the facts. I put forth this small history under a firm belief that it is due to those who acted, that their doings should be registered, and it is also proper that each coming generation should read and know what was done by its ancestors.

Take, read, and contrast the many privileges now enjoyed, compared with the many privations of the first settlers, and take encouragement to persevere.

In all the toils of this protracted undertaking, the author has been animated by the hope of offering an acceptable and useful service to the present and future generations, by detailing the elements from which has grown the prosperity and present happy condition of a free people.

N. B. NORTHROP.

MEDINA, JUNE, 1861.

Pioneer History of
Medina
County

OHIO

N. B. Northrop

HERITAGE BOOKS
2010

HERITAGE BOOKS
AN IMPRINT OF HERITAGE BOOKS, INC.

Books, CDs, and more—Worldwide

For our listing of thousands of titles see our website
at
www.HeritageBooks.com

A Facsimile Reprint
Published 2010 by
HERITAGE BOOKS, INC.
Publishing Division
100 Railroad Ave. #104
Westminster, Maryland 21157

Index Copyright © 1999 Heritage Books, Inc.

Entered, according to Act of Congress, in the year 1861, by N. B. Northrop, in the Clerk's Office of the District Court of the United States for the Northern District of Ohio

— Publisher's Notice —
In reprints such as this, it is often not possible to remove blemishes from the original. We feel the contents of this book warrant its reissue despite these blemishes and hope you will agree and read it with pleasure.

International Standard Book Numbers
Paperbound: 978-0-7884-1184-7
Clothbound: 978-0-7884-8330-1

WESTERN RESERVE.

THE WESTERN RESERVE, of which Medina county is a portion, is situated in the north-east quarter of the State, bounded north by Lake Erie, east by Pennsylvania, south by the parallel of the forty-first degree of north latitude, and west by the counties of Sandusky and Seneca. Its length east and west is 120 miles, by an average width of 50 miles from south to north, comprising an area of 3,800,000 acres. It is surveyed into townships of five miles square. A half million of acres was stricken off the west part, and donated by the State of Connecticut, to certain sufferers by fire, in the revolutionary war.

The manner by which Connecticut became possessed of that portion of Ohio, called the Western Reserve, was the following: King Charles 2nd, of England, granted to the Colony of Connecticut in 1662 a charter right to all lands included within certain specific boundaries. At that early period the geographical knowledge of Europeans concerning America was very limited. Patents that had been granted often interfered with each other and caused confusion and disputes. The charter granted to Connecticut by King Charles embraced all lands contained between the 41st and 42nd parallels of north latitude, and from Providence plantations on the east, to the Pacific Ocean on the west, with the exception of the New York and Pennsylvania colonies. For some years after the United States became an independent nation the interfering claims occasioned much collision of sentiment between the Union and the State of Connecticut. The controversy was, after many years, compromised by the United States relinquishing all their claim, and guaranteeing to the State of Connecticut the exclusive right of soil in the 3,800,000 acres as before described.

The United States, by the terms of the compromise, reserved to themselves the right of jurisdiction, and in due course of time they united the Western Reserve to the north-western territory, from which was created the State of Ohio.

Trumbull County was formed in 1800 and comprised in its limits, at that date, the whole of the Western Reserve. At that early date there were very few openings made or settlements between Warren and Sandusky. Portage was formed from Trumbull in 1807, and for two years the seat of justice was appointed at the house of Benj. Tappan, who settled in Ravenna in 1799. Medina was formed from Portage in 1818.

It may be a matter of interest to the reader to know the names of the first counties within what is now called the State of Ohio. The county of Washington was established in 1788, by Arthur St. Clair, then Governor of the territory, extending westward to the Scioto and northward to Lake Erie, embracing nearly one-half the present area of the State. In 1790 Hamilton County was established, embracing that portion of the State between the two Miamis, and extending north to a line drawn east from the standing forks of the great Miami. The County of Wayne was established in 1796, including within its boundaries the north-western portion of Ohio, part of north-eastern Indiana and the whole of Michigan territory. In July, 1797, Adams

County was established, comprehending a large tract of territory on each side of Scioto river, and extending north to the south line of the then Wayne County. Prior to 1798 the whole area now composing the State of Ohio was comprised within those four counties.

Medina County was formed February 18th, 1812, from that part of the Reserve west of the 11th range, south of number 5, and east of the 20th range, and attached to Portage County, until organized. It was organized in April, 1818. The first settlers of the county were principally from Connecticut, though within the last twenty years there has been a large accession of industrious Germans. The surface is rolling, with a larger portion of bottom than ridge land; the soil is generally clay and gravel loam, and is better adapted to the growth of grass than grain. The principal products are corn, oats, wheat, hay, butter and cheese.

The first settlement made within the present limits of the county, and prior to its organization, was at Harrisville, in February, 1811, by Joseph Harris and family, which was then composed of wife and one child.

Shortly thereafter a second settlement was made in Liverpool township, by Justus Warner. The war of 1812 having been commenced, caused delay in making settlements in other sections of the county, which continued for more than two years. After the close of the war in 1815, settlements became more numerous. The village now called Medina, was originally called Mecca, as can be seen on maps of an early date.

In 1814, Mr. Zenas Hamilton made an opening within that portion of the county called Medina Township. The want of a market caused the price of produce to be very low. Wheat was sold in 1820 for 25 cents and less per bushel, and more than one person in the county can tell of offering ten bushels of wheat for one pound of tea. A man hauled with oxen a wagon load of husked corn ten miles, with which to buy three yards of satinet for pantalets. Often did men attend church with woolen pants patched with buckskin. Ox teams were the pleasure carriages of the early settlers. Five yards would make a full dress for a lady who resided in what is now Medina County, in 1814.

The settlements in the county commenced in a manner that might seem peculiar. Instead of making openings on one side, or in some particular section of the county, and as they were strengthened by accession in numbers, they began their settlements wherever their individual interests led them. Many openings were made at the distance of many miles from each other. In consequence of the distance, journeys had frequently to be taken ten or fifteen miles for the sole purpose of getting some mechanical job done, which, though trifling in value, must be done in order to push forward business at home. In getting to and from mill, days were spent. For many years the nearest post-office was Cleveland, to which place a man would spend two days in going and returning, for sake of a single letter. Often have fathers left their families and started with ox team fifteen or twenty miles in quest of provision. The necessary outfit would be axe, blanket and bell. With axe, he cut his road, with blanket or quilt he was protected against inclement seasons, and bells told where to find his oxen when let loose to graze during the night. Where he tarried all night an unbroken wilderness was his inn, and the howling of wolves the nightly music to charm. At early dawn he arose, listened for the sound of the bell, got his trusty oxen yoked, ate his meal in silence, but with gratitude, rolled up his scanty bed-covering and traveled forward.

The young folks in an old settled country have a very faint knowledge of the daily hardships and privations endured by first settlers. To have a view of Medina County and its inhabitants, and contrast *then* and *now*, the change would be truly great. It was not uncommon in pioneer times to find a young man, with no implement but axe, engaged, solitary and alone, felling the forest and making the first opening. A rude hut, hastily constructed, was his dwelling, a piece of pork, a loaf of corn bread and a few potatoes his dainty and daily food. A pronged stick was his fork, a split slab his table, and a few leaves and a quilt his bed. There he toiled, there he cooked, ate, and slept soundly, for many weeks without seeing or conversing with any human being. At night when the rushing winds ceased to make the forest vocal, the wolves were the only tribe that serenaded him with their wild music.

After months of trial and privation, by the industry of the young man, the opening is made, the rude cabin erected, and thoughts of seeking and gaining a companion are entertained. The more comfortable homes of his nativity are revisited by him, his school-mate is thought upon, the future prospects in the western wilderness are portrayed, and in a few weeks the same young man who had lived alone becomes a husband, and in company with wife returns to his cabin.

To entertain his better half (using his own language) the bed must be reconstructed, and additional furniture and table ware must be provided. With axe and saw he made a bedstead, on which was placed a tow tick, filled with fall grass. A large pocket knife did all the carving, two short blocks were the chairs, and a puncheon, hewed by the axe was the table.

In process of time there were strong evidences that a little calico would be needed. To procure it the young husband travelled nine miles, but got there too late. All the calico was sold, and the merchant had not cloth of any kind that would make a little frock. He returned weary and disappointed to his home, and sorrowfully told his wife of his disappointment. The good wife informed him that she could make a pretty decent frock out of a pair of his old tow trousers.

In due time the little stranger came, and was furnished with the frock. Years came and went, the child became a man. The father and mother died, that son was heir, and in the course of 35 years from the first opening made by his father, he sold the farm for $1750, went to the west, where he now resides, surrounded with all that makes life agreeable.

To one of our modern belles, such a life would be intolerable. Let not such contemn. Their grand-mother used the spinning-wheel for a piano, a splint broom, made by her husband, swept the puncheon floor, and the ox team hauled her and family to church. Such pioneers are worthy of grateful remembrance.

Many now ride in carriages whose grand-father resided in cabins, the windows of which were constructed by cutting out a log, putting in slats perpendicularly and horizontally, and using paper greased with bear's oil or hog-lard instead of glass. Not a few of the early settlers ground their corn in a hand mill, or pounded it in a hommony block with the but end of an iron wedge. The finer part of the corn meal was used for bread, the coarser portion was used as hommony, which when boiled was considered by many delicious food.

COUNTY STATISTICS.

IN 1818 the county of Medina was organized. At the organization there were nineteen townships, comprising a larger area of land than at present—Norton, Copley, Bath, Richfield, Wadsworth, Granger, Hinckley, Guilford, Montville, Medina, Brunswick, Westfield, Liverpool, Harrisville, Grafton, Sullivan, Penfield and Huntington. In 1826 the lands listed and returned to the County Auditor for taxation were 411,904 acres; valued at 939,382 dollars, being a fraction more than two dollars per acre. In 1827 the townships of Grafton, Penfield, Huntington and Sullivan were taken to form in part the county of Lorain. After the detachment of the foregoing townships the number of acres in the county was cut down to 295,043, and listed for taxation at 719,078 dollars, being nearly three dollars per acre. From the year last named to 1830 very little change in the taxation of real estate occurred. In 1830 the townships of Sharon, Lafayette and York were organized, having been previously attached to contiguous townships. In 1831, '32 and '33 the townships that now compose the county were organized and recognized. Having given a hasty account of the original townships, I will now give in detail their valuations and taxes, and for the purpose of showing the progress and increase in value of each township, I will commence in 1826 and give an exhibit every five years:

COUNTY STATISTICS.

No. 1.

NAMES OF TOWNSHIPS, 1826.	Value of Lands.	Value of Personal Property	TAXES.
Norton, - - -	$50,136	$8,608	$597 06
Copley, - - -	40,419	2,820	410 96
Bath, - - -	36,415	2,376	368 57
Richfield, - - -	53,798	10,008	606 15
Wadsworth, - - -	42,350	6,360	462 74
Attached to Granger, (now Sharon,)	43,965	544	422 84
Granger, - - -	40,299	2,752	408 99
Hinckley, - - -	40,527	752	392 05
Guilford, - - -	38,179	2,340	384 74
Montville, - - -	37,392	992	379 05
Medina, - - -	34,779	7,076	413 30
County Plat, - - -	2,623		25 92
Brunswick, - - -	34,215	4,920	371 79
Westfield, - - -	29,608	3,400	313 58
Attached to Westfield, (now Lafayette,)	33,852		321 60
Attached to Medina, (now York,)	29,936		295 62
Liverpool, - - -	37,232	2,520	377 65
Harrisville, - - -	35,785	5,864	395 66
Attached to Harrisville, (now Chatham)	28,464		270 41
Attached to Grafton, (now Litchfield,)	26,885		255 41
Grafton, - - -	39,952	2,544	365 52
Attached to Sullivan, (now Homer.)	30,888		293 43
Sullivan, - - -	35,154	1,300	346·45
Attached to Penfield, (now Spencer,)	30,029		296 54
Penfield, - - -	29,433	1,240	302 80

Making a total value of real and personal property to be $1,006,453, and the taxes $9,664 97.

COUNTY STATISTICS.

Next is presented an account of the valuation of real and personal property, and the taxes on the same, for the year 1830:

No. 2.

NAMES OF TOWNSHIPS, 1830.	Value of Lands.	Value of Personal Property	TAXES.
Norton,	$47,449	$8,640	$603 36
Copley,	39,051	3,864	409 52
Bath,	37,340	2,952	382 79
Richfield,	54,068	8,040	620 36
Wadsworth,	44,280	11,568	554 68
Attached to Granger,	43,965		636 45
Granger,	40,441	4,952	593 87
Hinckley,	40,456	2,233	405 55
Guilford,	37,597	4,840	759 68
Montville,	37,184	1,656	396 82
Medina,	39,807	10,040	529 28
Brunswick,	36,066	6,264	728 46
Westfield,	30,599	4,312	363 43
Attached to Westfield,	34,826		330 86
Attached to Medina,	29,936		314 33
Liverpool,	37,687	4,168	397 93
Harrisville,	35,165	5,040	435 92
Attached to Harrisville,	28,102		395 70
Attached to Medina.	26,855		308 95

In the foregoing table the townships of Granger, Guilford and Brunswick had wisely allowed a tax to build school-houses to be assessed, which makes their payments seem large when contrasted with the valuation of other townships. A tax for road purposes, also, had been put on duplicate and aids to increase the tax.

COUNTY STATISTICS.

This table will present a different feature in valuation. Town Lots in Medina and Seville are being placed on duplicate. Town Lots and Buildings in Medina are valued at 20,829 dollars. Town Lots and Buildings in Seville are listed at 1,130 dollars. No other townships report any Town Lots. Merchants' Capital now becomes taxable and comprises a large item. The number of horses and cattle increases and swells the basis on which to levy. The price per acre of land is rising, and every item gives evidence of increasing wealth:

No. 3.

NAMES OF TOWNSHIPS, 1835.	Value of Lands and Houses.	Value of Personal Property	TAXES.
Norton,	$58,173	$19,615	$595 23
Copley,	58,810	11,924	671 91
Bath,	57,122	9,424	722 74
Richfield,	65,253	32,808	644 88
Wadsworth,	63,186	23,270	626 07
Sharon,	53,807	6,640	559 26
Granger,	50,979	9,976	685 51
Hinckley,	57,166	7,642	488 60
Guilford,	55,007	14,950	477 41
Montville,	52,868	6,718	498 77
Medina,	67,760	28,408	736 54
Brunswick,	53,523	16,844	640 92
Westfield,	47,919	13,154	431 77
Lafayette,	45,328	1,696	362 77
York,	42,410	2,816	332 52
Liverpool,	50,594	7,976	392 53
Harrisville,	37,524	11,6 0	325 65
Chatham,	43,243	1,384	525 69
Litchfield,	37,870	2,415	283 21

In this table the townships of Spencer and Homer are listed and assessed with the townships named. Although those two townships are formed and have elected township officers, their organization was not consummated in time to appear separately for taxation in 1835.

COUNTY STATISTICS. 15

Up to close of 1839 the townships of Norton, Copley, Bath and Richfield composed a part of Medina county. Thereafter they became a part of Summit county, taking off the duplicate a valuation of $177,908 of real estate, $23,496 of personal property, and $2,016 13 of tax. From 1840 onward the valuation and taxes in each township comprising the county can be given without being in any way mixed with parts of other counties:

No. 4.

NAMES OF TOWNSHIPS, 1840.	Value of Lands and Buildings	Value of Personal Property	TAXES.
Wadsworth, - - -	$66,322	$21,576	$1,002 63
Sharon, - - -	55,530	13,964	880 18
Granger, - - -	52,504	11,154	1,106 03
Hinckley, - -	56,458	9,894	974 24
Guilford, - - -	58,324	18,562	941 51
Montville, - -	52,842	14,756	1,265 46
Medina, - - -	78,592	25,836	1,729 41
Brunswick, - -	55,268	13,076	1,045 16
Westfield, - . .	45,356	7,120	766 11
Lafayette, - -	51,756	16,036	802 61
York, - - -	43,944	9,038	776 65
Liverpool, - -	52,882	10,264	1,008 78
Harrisville, - - -	41,006	18,896	757 13
Chatham, - -	44,320	5,322	1,321 34
Litchfield, - - -	38,966	6,752	608 22
Homer, - - -	42,812	4,440	693 51
Spencer, - - -	43,545	5,051	690 29

In some of the townships there had been levied heavy taxes for road, township and school-house purposes, that may seem to the observer disproportionate when observing the valuation.

COUNTY STATISTICS.

In the following table there is a marked increase of personal estate placed on duplicate for taxation, and still the taxes increase:

No. 5.

NAMES OF TOWNSHIPS, 1845.	Value of Lands and Buildings	Value of Personal Property	TAXES.
Wadsworth,	$62,309	$31,149	$1,424 94
Sharon,	58,112	19,163	1,282 79
Granger,	52,434	14,776	1,085 06
Hinckley,	53,110	16,201	1,450 56
Guilford,	60,719	32,215	1,402 54
Montville,	56,139	18,264	1,030 50
Medina,	71,314	36,063	1,976 18
Brunswick,	54,721	19,563	1,812 53
Westfield,	47,621	26,152	1,076 19
Lafayette,	44,063	15,138	956 44
York,	42,912	13,954	869 74
Liverpool,	50,735	18,402	1,101 20
Harrisville,	46,331	29,528	1,159 39
Chatham,	42,335	11,487	873 79
Litchfield,	40,576	11,940	753 14
Homer,	33,710	11,140	673 45
Spencer,	38,221	21,706	823 65

COUNTY STATISTICS.

Another valuation of real estate being made, and many other articles of personal property being, by law, brought on duplicate, necessarily makes a much larger valuation. Although there are only the same number of acres of land it must be remembered that the price, per acre, is greater, and that the erection of comfortable and necessary buildings has increased the value of the farms:

No. 6.

NAMES OF TOWNSHIPS, 1850.	Value of Lands and Buildings	Value of Personal Property	TAXES.
Wadsworth,	$271,102	$77,226	$2,034 56
Sharon,	244,582	43,250	1,728 64
Granger,	172,4;0	48,090	1,498 14
Hinckley,	196,118	42,222	1,831 02
Guilford,	240,684	63,852	1,991 53
Montville,	212,040	51,870	1,619 87
Medina,	235,188	76,846	2,220 00
Brunswick,	191,172	60,472	1,787 63
Westfield,	195,104	37,514	1,296 36
Lafayette,	171,404	35,706	1,330 45
York,	174,200	33,060	1,344 74
Liverpool,	186,276	57,368	1,516 97
Harrisville,	189,254	73,752	1,427 95
Chatham,	152,100	44,956	1,377 55
Litchfield,	159,638	35,550	1,081 00
Homer,	127,340	24,208	947 64
Spencer,	137,976	41,906	1,194 66

COUNTY STATISTICS.

The following table presents a marked increase in the valuation of real estate and double the value of personal property. Why the taxes should have more than doubled within five years may create suspicions in the minds of those who doubt much, yet it is easy to demonstrate that the increase of taxes originates in townships. Of the taxes reported in the following table $7,800 were ordered to be levied by township trustees for road purposes:

No. 7.

NAMES OF TOWNSHIPS, 1855.	Value of Lands and Building	Value of Personal Property	TAXES.
Wadsworth, - - -	$480,544	$159,008	$3,951 14
Sharon, - - -	407,940	119,432	3,455 79
Granger, - - -	325,400	75,474	2,755 27
Hinckley, - -	340,326	107,780	3,511 93
Guilford, - - -	427,348	195,574	4,398 16
Montville, - -	366,552	114,914	2,858 60
Medina, - - -	422,192	246,398	5,317 90
Brunswick, - -	333,674	108,512	4,047 04
Westfield, - - -	325,060	100,050	3,108 16
Lafayette, - -	336,738	90,154	3.291 73
York, - - -	335,030	82,856	2,823 62
Liverpool, - -	372,118	144,424	3,622 72
Harrisville, - - -	185,746	154,048	3,400 90
Chatham, - -	269,672	87,884	2,637 95
Litchfield, - - -	251,584	67,928	2,773 98
Homer, - - -	244,674	84,490	2,466 10
Spencer, - - -	282,224	102,920	2,608 56

COUNTY STATISTICS.

This table gives the taxes of 1860, as made out and charged against the several townships:

No. 8.

NAMES OF TOWNSHIPS, 1860.	Value of Lands and Buildings	Value of Personal Property	TAXES.
Wadsworth,	$415,956	$153,404	$4,431 07
Sharon,	356,386	129,336	4,077 87
Granger,	314,508	104,910	4,332 42
Hinckley,	357,092	100,828	4,084 19
Guilford,	405,738	203,952	5,485 29
Montville,	342,812	120,740	4,173 22
Medina,	358,692	225,012	6,667 72
Brunswick,	324,452	98,350	3,934 74
Westfield,	341,976	99,184	3,511 24
Lafayette,	304,864	109,042	3,439 42
York,	251,110	85,514	3,158 98
Liverpool.	343,190	109,690	3,904 78
Harrisville,	343,666	156,270	4,129 09
Chatham,	336,550	129,470	4,439 49
Litchfield,	283,854	87,214	3,850 96
Homer,	287,700	'4,722	3,042 13
Spencer,	326,754	115,766	3,950 13

COUNTY STATISTICS.

The following table, compiled from the statistics of 1850, will give an imperfect estimate of the value of the county:

Value of Lands,		$4,732,650
"	Farm Implements and Machinery,	210,575
"	Live Stock,	762,758
"	Wheat,	132,446
"	Corn,	104,560
"	Oats,	41,216
"	Wool,	91,980
"	Potatoes,	10,644
"	Orchard Fruits,	14,800
"	Butter,	61,880
"	Cheese,	14,800
"	Cloverseed,	15,260
"	Maple Sugar,	23,866
"	Home Manufactures,	6,699
Making a total in 1850 of		6,243,452
Since that date the increase in value has been		1,248,710
Making the value in 1860 to be		7,492,262

Another item that adds to the yearly wealth is the actual value of churches. A list with the value of that kind of property is here appended:

6 Baptist Churches, valued at		$7,000
11 Congregational Churches, valued at		12,000
1 Episcopal	" "	2,000
2 Lutheran	" "	800
18 Methodist	" "	9,700
4 Presbyterian	" "	5,200
2 Roman Catholic	" "	1,750
2 Universalist	" "	2,400
Total value of Church Property		38,850

Adding the sources enumerated to the untold minor founts from which small but continued rills of wealth yearly issue, there is no hazard in stating that the wealth

COUNTY STATISTICS.

of Medina county in 1860 amounts to *ten millions*. If the present generation will carefully reflect upon the meagre sources of wealth enjoyed in 1818, and contrast them with the present, they must be convinced that *industry* and *economy* are the channels in which permanent wealth flows.

SCHOOLS.

It is interesting to notice the advances made in the cause of Education. Prior to 1836, but little aid accrued from legal enactments. For a period of 20 years the schools were in a great measure sustained by subscription, and the houses where the children congregated rudely constructed. Now, every township is furnished with educational buildings that give evidence of the progress of Christian civilization.

To show the contrast in this particular between 1818 and 1860, the following table is compiled:

Value of School-Houses in 1818, (37 in number,) -		$1.480
" " 1860, (124 in number,) -		34,200
Amount paid teachers in 1818, - - - -		3,700
" " 1860, - - - -		15,208
No. of youth attending school in 1818,	- -	620
" " 1860,	- -	4,782

In addition to the foregoing, there are now in successful progress at least eight High Schools or Academies, which are doing a good work for the youth of the county. During the Autumn and Winter months, the duty of managing the common schools is entrusted to males — during Spring and Summer, to females.

COUNTY STATISTICS.

INCREASE OF POPULATION.

The correct number of inhabitants in each township in 1818 can only be learned from persons then residents, but it is presumed to be tolerably reliable. The population, by townships, for 1860, is given as returned by the Deputy Marshal:

TOWNSHIPS.	Population, 1818.	Population, 1860.
Wadsworth,	227	1,703
Lafayette,	91	1,327
Montville,	87	951
Medina,	163	968
Medina Village,	118	1,220
Sharon,	96	1,313
Brunswick,	167	1,267
Liverpool,	219	1,891
Hinckley,	118	1,227
Guilford,	209	1 825
Westfield,	79	1,122
Harrisville,	231	1,226
Chatham,	107	1,156
Spencer,	81	1,083
Homer,	72	993
Granger,	184	1,025
Litchfield,	96	1,117
York,	124	1.070
Total,	2,469	22,484

THE FIRST COURT.

The following narrative is from the pen of Mr. James Moore, of Diamond Lake, Illinois, who was for many years, prior to his removal, a resident of Medina, and was one of the first Pioneers of the Township.

January 14th, 1818, the county of Medina was set apart from Portage county and organized, and, as well as I can recollect, provision made for holding court the June following; a Barn, erected by Esq. Ferris, within the present limits of the corporation, was selected as the most suitable place, preparations were made, and the scales of Justice were raised, and the rights of the straw eating ox for a while were lost in the exaltation of his humble stall, where reason and justice were to meet. The Court consisted of George Todd, of Trumbull County, as President, Messrs. Harris, of Harrisville, Brown, of Wadsworth, and Welton, of Richfield, the associate part of the court. On the day appointed a full court assembled, and the citizens generally turned out to see the working of this intellectual mill. In these days men did their own logrolling; we had the genuine article then, and enough of it. The Sheriff had announced the court as open, and for litigants to draw near and they should be heard, but as there was nothing to be litigated the court adjourned till next day. The day wore away in friendly greetings and social chat. The Exodus of the Eastern states was showering in upon us, and the sound of the axe in all directions gave evidence of the fact, and after a good supper at Esq. Ferris' the Pioneer unlocked his store of adventure, (to wit;) his deer or wolf hunt, success in treating the murrian death, as well as hair breadth escapes from falling trees, or an occasional sally from Guy Boughton, who assured the company that the last freshet in Black river had destroyed the nesting places of the Bank swallow and left the holes sticking out several feet. But time, that waits for no one, brought the hour of repose, when some twenty or thirty of us repaired to the barn (Court House) and in military parlance were resting upon our arms when Esq. Ferris with lights, decanters, and a reinforcement of several persons arrived, and, in the blandest manner possible, observed it was with extreme regret he could furnish no better lodging but, as it was, he had a great substitute for feathers, and invited all who were about to sleep by the Job to come forward and take a little comfort from the decanters. This advice was considered good, and in a short time the decanters were empty, and before the Esq. returned with replenished decanters conversation had taken a stride, listeners had become speakers, and, by the time the decanters had been filled the third time, some three or four persons had mounted the Judge's table, each a different subject and vociferating at the full strength of his lungs. Those on the floor, of more humble pretentions, were essaying extempore verse, with a full chorus of "One Bottle More," "One Bottle More." In this crisis Doct. B. B. Clark, was called in professionally, and at once decided that alarming symptoms did show themselves, a mighty disease was in progress, and, although local in its inception, would in the end prove highly contagious, as well as fatal, as several had already passed into a collapsed state of the disease. The Doctor recommended tonics in large doses, and with two persons at each arm; with one to steady the head several potions were given with great effect. Several of the patients became skeptical as to the newtonian law of gravitation, for with them the barn (Court House,) rocked on its foundation; with others the lights mysteriously receded, and sounds fell on the auditory that no language can portray. In this distress, as a substitute for electricity, a dry cow-skin was procured, and several of the patients were elevated some three or four feet and suffered to descend by their own weight. This had a great effect and was considered at the time an improvement in the treatment of this disease. At breakfast the next morning several of the worst cases were convalescent, a great proof that the treatment was based on scientific research, and it was hoped the worst was over; but it was whispered at breakfast there had been a Riot last night, the peace and dignity of the Court and State had been outraged, and something must be done as a terror to evil doers; but on further inquiry it was found that a portion of the Court had strong symptoms of the disease, and that a change of venue would be awarded the Riotors. You are aware that a house divided against itself cannot stand. So ended the first Court in the county of Medina.

THE EARLY SETTLERS.

Ye favored young people, no perils so rare,
Can the writers of romance ever prepare,
As those that imperil'd your parents so dear,
Who came to these wilds when the woods were all here;
Cast the lords of the forest down to the tomb,
From hills where your gardens and orchards now bloom;
Built up the abodes where in peace you abide,
And founded the temples 'neath which you reside.

Privations and hardships, toils and temptations,
Attended their steps and haunted their stations;
Their cattle ran wild in the forest away,
For the wolves, for bears and for panthers a prey;
The wild cat and wolf, the panther and owl,
Around their rude dwellings at midnight would howl;
And serpents most deadly while seeking the sun,
Would creep out and sleep on their thresholds at noon.

THE EARLY SETTLERS.

A few of the Fathers so noble and brave,
Are still lingering with us this side of the grave,
And we to their deeds a just tribute would pay,
E're they from our presence have all passed away;
The signet of truth in their life is set well,
Or we could not believe the stories they tell
Respecting the changes that around them appear,
Wrought out from the forest that they once saw here:

And we question if they can fully believe,
The things that their senses so fully perceive.
Let them look at highways now leading about,
In contrast with the roads on which they came out,
Winding out then in a single direction;
Running round now to ev'ry mile section;
Guided then by spots on the trees blazed awide;
Guarded now by fences along either side.

Then full of turns, roots and holes, everywhere:
Now, straight, well bridged, cast up and graded with care;
Now, the carriage with wheels glides smoothly away;
Then, 'twas lifting, tipping and plunging all day:
Now, straight, smooth iron roads are much in employ;
Then, our mi'ry swamps were bridged with corduroy;
Then, ten miles a days was oft with hardship won;
Now, five hundred miles a day are easy run.

THE EARLY SETTLERS.

Then, the household came West with oxen for team ;
Now, horses of iron bring whole hamlets by steam :
Then, letters were brought by codgers in their shoes ;
Now, outspeeding light, the lightning brings us news;
Then, rocky New England, the land of their birth
Seemed lost in the distance far o'er the broad earth ;
Now, a few hours ride brings her hills into view,
And restores them to scenes their infancy knew.

Then, scarce a dwelling by the wayside appeared ;
Now, hamlet and cot on all sides are reared.
Then, not a free school in the region was found ;
Now, thousands of schools in the country abound :
Then, not a church appeared in the forest forlorn;
Now, hundreds of temples our hill sides adorn :
Then, not a trader life's comforts exchanged here ;
Now, millions of treasures are changed every year.

Then, the Early Settler was deemed half mad or wild,
Now 'tis famous to be an early settler's child :
Then, Emigrants in burlesque hung in Eastern halls ;
Now portraits of our veteran settlers grace those walls;
Then they said, go and come again in rags forlorn ;
Now they say, send us wheat and wool and fruit and corn;
Then men went back and said this was a cursed state ;
Now Heaven and Earth proclaim it both good and great;

THE EARLY SETTLERS.

Now, Fathers, in view of these contrasts, can you
Comprehend the change in this country so new?
Are you the men that in young manhood came here
This wilderness world of its wildness to clear?
Does your reason retain your identity fast
Amid all the changes through which you have past?
Can your memory recall the work of each year,
Since you came to this land a rough pioneer?

But who can describe all the hues of your care,
As you struggle in want, almost in dispair,
To shelter, feed and clothe your family charge,
And shield them from evils that threaten at large:
Who can describe the patient toils of the wife,
The stitches and tables she's set in her life:
The cares of the mother what pen can portray,
Wearing, grinding her heart, by night and by day.

The steps and strokes required the household to rear,
Can only be told when books from Heaven appear.
Husbands, love your wives, the Holy Scripture saith:
Look at your wife as she toils from breath to breath;
Once a day she's swept your house and made your bed;
Three times a day food prepared and table spread:
Three times a day dishes brought your meals to grace;
Three times a day dishes washed and put in place.

Day after day to the milk and butter seen ;
Week after week she's washed your floors and linen clean;
Mop't the floors in spots, perhaps ten times as oft ;
Spun and wove, may be, most of your raiments soft :
Made and patched your shirts and pants, coat and vest :
The sheets and quilts with which your couch is drest :
Knit and darned your socks with stitch and step beside,
Toiling breath by breath some comfort to provide.

But now her step is feeble, and her head is white,
And still your highest comfort is her delight :
Two score years perhaps and ten she's been your wife,
Your delight the greatest comfort of her life :
More than eighteen thousand times she's made your bed,
And fifty-four thousand times your table spread ;
Sadly watched your couch in weary hours of pain,
Gladly seen you rise to health and strength again.

Now what poet can describe or ready writer tell,
The hoping and fearing, seeing and hearing,
Seeking and finding, loosing and binding,
Wooing and wedding, quilting and bedding,
Spinning and weaving, coming and leaving,
Wearing and tearing, dividing and sharing,
Patching and mending, calling and sending,
The borrowing and lending.

THE EARLY SETTLERS.

The staying and going, knitting and sewing.
Washing and baking, sweating and shaking,
Toasting and stewing, roasting and brewing,
Toasting and smelling, buying and selling,
Grinding and sifting, tugging and lifting,
Skimming and churning, greasing and turning,
Stirring and beating, cooling and eating,
Setting and cleaning.

The slashing and logging, ditching and bogging,
Shifting and turning, piling and burning,
Digging and hoeing, plowing and sowing,
Threshing and reaping, carting and heaping,
Stocking and seeding, mowing and feeding,
Hewing and scoring, marking and boring,
Loading and drawing, planing and sawing,
The salving and swathing, nursing and bathing.

The sobbing and sighing, laughing and crying,
Hugging and squeezing, tewing and teasing,
Telling and teaching, singing and preaching,
The scolding and spanking, the praying and thanking,
And many other things beyond my power to name,
That with the founding of these loving households came;
I ask you all ye living men, what pen can tell,
The toils and cares that on these households fell.

BRUNSWICK.

BY EPHRAIM LINDLEY.

In giving a detail of my pioneer life I may use words that may seem strange, perhaps offensive, to many of the present day. I was not raised in the lap of plenty nor educated in the school of refinement. I was born in Ira, Rutland county, Vermont, in 1796. In 1803 my father moved to Bristol, Hartford county, Connecticut, to take charge of the farm of his aged and infirm parents—a region of country once noted for clock-making and various other arts carried on by machinery. While living at Bristol I commenced attending school, and to give some idea of my young thoughnts on good manners, I will relate a school adventure. A boy called Charles Bartholomew, during the absence of the teacher from the schoolroom, thought proper to leave his seat and come and sit facing me in what I considered a very saucy manner. Feeling my dignity insulted by his continued gaze, and believing him to be a violator of good order and of the rules of the school, in the absence of the teacher, I laid down my book, walked up to Charles, gave him a severe slap on the side of the head and authoritatively ordered him to return to his seat and attend to his studies. Soon the teacher came in and seeing Charles crying inquired the cause. Being informed that that *new scholar* (meaning me,) had slapped him because he had neglected his studies, the teacher kindly addressed herself to me and informed me that it was contrary to the rules of her school for one scholar to correct another, and I got clear of correction under the plea that I was *new*. Once I saw a great gnat biting a comrade in school, and feeling full of sport I raised my hand, aimed a blow at the gnat with the force that felled my schoolmate to the floor. Upon being interrogated why I struck the boy, my answer was, that I would not stand still and see such a contemptible little insect as a gnat sucking blood from a comrade without using means to kill it. My laconic answer shielded me, that time, from merited chastisement.

After the decease of my grandfather and the apportionment of his estate among heirs, my father was persuaded by my uncle, Eliada Lindley, to move to Ohio. On 4th July, 1811, we left Bristol. We had an ox team headed by one horse. We toiled and traveled over rough roads, mud, and the many obstacles that had then to be encountered, until we came to the Cataraugus Swamp, where we were compelled to hire an additional force of horses, and a man to drive. Though the distance across that swamp was only four miles, yet we were a whole day getting over. After a toilsome journey of two months we arrived at Hudson.

Soon after our arrival in the then wilderness, intelligence of war greeted our ears often and sadly. After the surrender of Hull, many were forced to prepare for the tented field, who were very poorly supplied with the necessaries of life. The whole country was new—provisions were scarce and very high in price, and laborers few. Danger and privation were dreaded and experienced. Salt, one of the real necessities, was high in price and very scarce. A neighbor had been at

Liverpool and had got all the salt he contracted for, except one peck, which he said my father might have if he would send for it. The offer was considered a great accomodation, and my father selected me as the person who should go to Liverpool, a distance of 25 miles, for the peck of salt. I was then 16 years old. An empty sack was got, in which was stowed bread and wild meat, and on a cold blustering morning in the month of December, 1813, I left Hudson for Liverpool. There was a blazed road from Hudson to Richfield. From thence I had to go to the north line of the township, and from thence find my way by blazed trees to Timothy Doan's, in Columbia. Between the house of widow Payne (Brecksville) and Mr. Doan's was an unbroken wilderness of 15 miles, excepting the blazed line made by surveyors. My first day's travel brought me to the cabin of Mrs. Payne. On the second day I got to Liverpool Salt works, took possession of the peck of salt and learned that I could buy another peck which I willingly purchased. I shouldered my half bushel of salt on the afternoon of the second day, and with elastic step started, homeward bound. The second night I tarried at the house of Horace Gunn, who lived near Thos. Doan's. Liverpool salt dripped much, and my own exercise causing sweat, the two came in contact and kept me uncomfortable. The next morning after leaving Mr. Gunn's, I had to repass through the 15 miles of continued wilderness, with a short allowance of bread, laded with a half bushel of wet salt. The snow was about four inches in depth. After I had passed over about two miles of my lonely forest road I met a company of wolves, who seemed to be on the track I made when going to Liverpool. In passing along, I discovered that they followed, though at respectful distance. There were five in number, and their frequent stopping and pawing in the snow caused me to conjecture that they meditated an attack. I furnished myself with a stout club and felt determined to tree and fight if they should attack me. After following for a distance of five miles or more they left keeping company and I traveled on very well satisfied with their absence. I am of the opinion that the bitterings of the salt and my own sweat was what they scented and prompted them to follow me. I got home safely with what remained of my half bushel of salt after a full share of bitterings had eked out. This was my first important errand, and I can assure you that I then traveled that distance and carried the salt more willingly than a young man of 16 years will now carry a half bushel of potatoes from the grocery to his home.

EARLY SETTLERS.

Solomon Harvey, James Stearn and Henry Parker were the first settlers in Brunswick in the months of October and November, 1815. Shortly after, Samuel Tillotson and family came in. The next was W. P. Stevens and family. On March 4, 1815, Solomon and Frederick Deming with their families settled. During the summer of the same year, John Hulet, Seymour Chapin, John Stearn, Andrew Deming and Henry Bogue with their families came in. In 1817, Jacob Ward, Rhoda Stowe, Harvey Stebbins, John Freese, B. W. Freese, W. Root, Seth Blood, L. Thayer, P. Clark, Peter, John and A. Berdan and others came and settled in various parts of the township. In 1818, the noise of the axe could be heard during the hours of labor in various parts of the township, and the smoke rising from the hastily constructed cabins gave proof that settlements were rapidly increasing. The hum of industry could be heard and seen as the wilderness gradually yielded.

DEATHS OF EARLY SETTLERS.

Of those who braved the toils and privations incident to a Pioneer life, and who aided each other in making the full sunshine upon the long bedimmed surface the following are deceased:

George W. Baldwin and wife,
C. Stearns " "
Seymour Knox " "
Darius Francis " "
Peter Berdan " "
Frederick Root " "

Of those enumerated among the early marriages, the following, at the close of more than 40 years, are still husband and wife. To them it is a pleasure to see the changes that have taken place since they wedded:

Abram Freese and wife,
Ephraim Lindley " "
James Stearns " "
Daniel Stearns " "
Harvey Stebbins " "
Jacob Ward " "
Isaac Ward " "
Horace Root " "
Wm. Root " "

From these aged individuals the inquirers after the history of the first settlers can gather information that would be perused with interest fifty years hence. They are the living witnesses of occurrences worthy of record.

DIED AT A GOOD OLD AGE.

To give evidence that industry and daily toil tends not to cut short our days, I here give names and age of Pioneer Fathers and mothers. Those of the first settlers yet living can attest the truth of my remark when they read the names.

John Ward, deceased at the age of	92	years,
Elizabeth Ward " "	89	"
John Stearns " "	92	"
Lucy Stearns " "	76	"
W. P. Stearns " "	87	"
Lydia Stearns " "	69	"
Persis Kingsbury " "	65	"
Samuel Tillotson " "	91	"
Sarah Tillotson " "	77	"
Solomon Deming " "	85	"
Roxanna Deming " "	66	"
John Hulet " "	86	"
Ephraim Fletcher " "	74	"
Jabez Kingsbury " "	80	"
Daniel Bogue " "	72	"

Making an average age of 80 years to each one named. It is not probable that any fourteen descendants of those named will, when deceased, be able to have it noted that they had lived so long. The increase of idleness and the various and varied kind of dissipation adopted and practised must enfeeble and shorten life. Industry is a physician that produces health, creates wealth, secures comfort, dispels gloom and lengthens life. Indolence brings want, discontent, and tends to shorten life.

BURYING GROUND.

Capt. John Stearns, who was the owner of about thirteen hundred acres of land, being advanced in years and wishing to provide for the future, generously donated two acres to be used as a Burying Ground for the township, and requested the citizens to meet and clear off a portion of the lot, that it might be used for that purpose when needed. The citizens generally sanctioned the proposition, and soon was heard the sound of axe and falling of forest trees. In a few days a portion was cleared, and now is the resting place of many, young and old, who once lived. In that lot the bodies of the first resident settlers were one after another deposited, and here and there can be read upon headstones the names of many who once labored actively to tame the wilderness.

ROADS.

For several years prior to the erection of Medina county, the establishment of roads was unsettled. Each settler undertook to make a road to suit his own convenience, and not unfrequently he joined with his next neighbor, in opening a way that could be of mutual advantage. The making of bridges generally called together the whole force of the then sparse community, and many days would be wholly devoted to construct

BRUNSWICK.

a bridge that would probably be carried away by a succeeding freshet. After the organization of the county, small appropriations were made for opening roads and making bridges. As cash was then scarce, a man would work at road-making from rising to setting sun for fifty cents and board himself.

It was much easier to get timber necessary for a bridge to the allotted spot than to get the logs placed. Ox teams were used in hauling, but rendered little aid in placing timbers. Rocky River was the largest stream meandering through several of the newly settled townships, and the intercourse between small settlements forced the inhabitants, as a matter of convenience, to decide upon places and unitedly aid in building bridges for general accommodation. Many of the first settlers spent days at their own expense and did not consider it oppressive. It was no uncommon act to see all the men in a community congregated early, and without stockings or shoes, laboring all day in water fixing abutments and placing the long heavy stringers thereon. As puncheons were used for flooring in nearly every dwelling, they were considered equally good for bridging. No saw-mills were erected when settlements first commenced, therefore the necessity of using puncheon and clapboards. It is not hazardous to say that in 1815 and for five years thereafter, five men actually performed more labor on roads than twenty men did in 1860. Necessity forced them to be industrious and their future prospects urged them to labor. It was not unusual for the men, while engaged in putting up a bridge, to see their wives issuing from the wilderness from various directions, laded with cooked provisions intended for those employed in bridge-making. It was not unusual for the mothers in the days of first settling to travel two or three miles laded with provisions for their husbands who would necessarily lose time if compelled to go to their dwellings for their dinners. The present generation would consider such an undertaking too wearisome and too hazardous. Few of the modern females would be willing to travel three or four miles to hunt the cows once each day, as was the practice among the families of early settlers.

In my details of the first openings and settlements made in the township of Brunswick, I may wholly fail to please those who feed on refined literature. It has always been my fortune (some would say misfortune) to gain a competence by industry, and to be measurably deprived of spending much time in reading. I have enjoyed a full share of the toils of life without many of the luxuries.

FIRST ELECTION.

On 6th April, 1818, the first election was held and the following comprised all the legal voters then in the township, to wit: John Stearns, Solomon Deming, John Hulet, Harvey Stebbins, Jacob Ward, Thomas Stearns, Andrew Deming, Joel Curtis, Elijah Hull, Henry Bogue, Ephraim Lindley, James Stearns, George J. Baldwin, Solomon Harvey, Horace Root, Darius Francis, Henry Parker, Daniel Stearns and John Hulet, Jr. Nineteen votes were polled that day, and it was considered a large election.

John Hulet, John Stearns and Solomon Deming were elected trustees; Darius Francis, Treasurer; Henry Parker, Constable; John Stearns and Jacob Ward, Justices of the Peace.

BRUNSWICK. 41

Nearly all the parents who first settled in the township had been members of some one of the christian churches in their native State, which they failed not to exhibit and practice in their wilderness cabins. Sectarian feelings were not cherished as now; but when Sabbath came, Episcopalians, Congregationalists, Methodists and other denominations united and held religious meetings. At the first religious meetings, citizens from Liverpool and Brunswick united. When meeting was held at William Warner's cabin, Justus Warner, who was an Episcopalian, took the lead in meeting, and when in Brunswick the leader of religious exercises was of the Methodist or Congregational denomination. Generally the small family dwelling was filled with those who revered the sabbath and church duties. The exercises commenced with singing, in which all took part, and were able to keep time and sing in unison without the aid of organ or other musical instrument. After singing, prayer devout and fervent was offered, then a sermon was read, one or more exhorted, then closed by singing. Many of those who witnessed those religious exercises in the then wilderness cannot have forgotten the zeal, the good feeling, the solemnity that was apparent. God smiled graciously on the first settlers and conferred upon them many and rich blessings while employed in rearing homes in the then wilderness. At the sabbath prayer-meetings there was a marked reverence and not a few can date back to those times and places their first and lasting religious impression. It was at one of those meetings the writer of this narrative felt convinced of his sins and resolved thereafter to seek, by intercession, the pardon of his sins and live a new life. With pleasure, thankfulness and gratitude he looks back to the time when God, by his Spirit, showed to him the beauty of the christian religion.

CAN A BUILDING BE RAISED WITHOUT WHISKEY?

In pioneer days it was a universal practice to furnish whiskey at house or barn raisings; and though few drank to excess, yet at raisings, ministers, deacons and church-members would participate in drinking, and not unfrequently one or more could be seen staggering and not fully able to set and keep their feet properly. Capt. John Stearns had got every thing in readiness and had fixed upon a day to raise his new barn, when it was discovered that no whiskey could be bought or even borrowed in the township, and more unfortunate still, that none could be had nearer than Talmadge. To go to that place and return would require two days. Mr. Stearns made known the matter to some of his neighbors who told him that under the present circumstances they thought perhaps the barn might be raised, though they could not fully approve of his course in not seeing about the whiskey sooner. On the day appointed, the people assembled, went to work, raised the barn and from that circumstance made the wise discovery that a building could be safely and speedily built without the use of whiskey.

FIRST SLEIGHING VISIT.

The young folks in Brunswick desiring to form the acquaintance of those of their age in other townships, concluded to visit the family of Rufus Ferris, who then lived north from the present County seat. Each young man got his female partner, and rigging jumpers made of long poles that answered for runners and thills, we fastened on a few boards on which we sat and traveled. Our road was marked out by blazed trees. We started

BRUNSWICK.   43

from what is now Brunswick center, and following the
blazed trees we got to Weymouth safely; from thence
by some kind of marks we got to the Joseph Northrop
farm where we crossed Rocky River and from there to
the cabin of Rufus Ferris. We tarried there engaged
in youthful sport until a late hour, and then started
home by the same road we had got there. A whole
night was spent in paying that visit. We then had no
buffalo robes to protect us from the storm. A bed quilt
was the traveling robe used in those days, and while
thus clad, the young ladies of those days considered
themselves fashionably protected against inclemency of
the season. A log across our path was not considered
an obstacle of great moment, neither did we consider
it a great detriment if hats or bonnets were taken from
our heads by hanging limbs. We considered the distance from Brunswick by way of Weymouth, to the
residence of Mr. Ferris but a short distance, and while
there partaking of his hospitality we considered ourselves well accommodated if chairs could be furnished
for one-half of our company. We went to pay a friendly
visit, not to seek out matters about which to sneer
thereafter. We were one portion of a wilderness family going in kindness to visit another. Our meetings
in those times, were characterized by friendship and
solicitude for each other's welfare and comfort.

CHURCH ORGANIZATONS.

Although no original records exist, there are living
witnesses to testify that the Methodist Episcopal Church
organized in April, 1817, and that Jacob Ward was
instrumental in procuring the organization. The first
members of that church were Jacob Ward, Rhoda

Stowe, John and Lucy Stearns, John and Hannah Hulet, Samuel and Sarah Tillotson, Thomas and Phebe Stearns, Polly Harvey, Lydia Crittenden and Olivia Ashley. The last two named then resided in Grafton, the others resided in Brunswick. Of the first founders of that church the following yet live: Jacob Ward, Hannah Hulet and Mrs. Hurlbert (formerly Lydia Crittenden.)

The Congregational Church was organized Febuary 19, 1819, by Reverends Simeon Woodruff and William Hanford, then acting missionaries. The names of those who united at the organization were Jabez and Persis Kingsbury, Andrew Deming, Fredrick Deming, Roxanna Deming, William P. and Lydia Stearns, Geo. J. and Nancy Baldwin, Lydia Woodbridge and Clarissa Stearns. Of the above not one is now living.

It was the general practice for all to be seen at one church when there failed to be preachers, on the same day, for each denomination. Disputations on doctrinal points were few and far between among the members of those churches. The gospel was preached and listened to, with due attention. All were neighbors, friends and brethren. The Episcopal Methodists erected the first meeting-house, the Congregationalists the second. As the members of each denomination had often prayed together, and often listened to the same preacher; with the same christian feeling they mutually aided each other in erecting church edifices.

SCHOOL HOUSES.

The first school house was erected on the west line of Brunswick in order to give accommodation to families in Liverpool township. Sarah Tillotson was the teacher, and her school in 1817 numbered 16 scholars. The second school house was built one-fourth of a mile west from the center, in the fall of 1817, and Col. John Freese was the teacher during the following winter. The third public building was built, by subscription, of hewed timber at the center, and was used for school, religious and town purposes. Could the young students of this day be permitted to look back forty years and view the narrow paths that led to the school houses where their fathers and mothers congregated, the rude building in which they, when children assembled, the rough and uncomfortable seats, the puncheon floor and the dim lights afforded, he would certainly be led to ask himself who accomplished the great change between *now* and *then*? No greater evidence of progress can be seen than to contrast the present educational facilities with those that the first settlers possessed. What great, profitable and good changes may not take place in the coming forty years if untiring perseverance be exercised, and our aim to elevate be observed?

LOUNGERS.

In pioneer days there were neither loungers nor lounging places. Every person, young or old had some profitable employment in which to engage. There were no groups of the idle or indolent to be seen standing or sitting at corners or stores, taverns or groceries. For many years after the first settlers came, in smokers of cigar or pipe were seldom seen. If the last ten years had been as profitably employed as were the first ten years from and after the first openings made by the original settlers, an improvement would have been

made in morals, in physical power, in agriculture and
in wealth. Degeneracy, in many things, has taken the
place of refinement, and many, too many, are reared
wholly untrained in any useful, necessary or profitable
employment. To make a contrast I will, in old fash-
ioned poetry, give you a description of a modern
lounger:

Our now-a-day loungers I'll describe, now I'm for it,
And in doing the same I'll ask them no pay for it;
If I charged them Dr., I should suffer a loss,
For the scamps are too mean to pay what it costs.
To tell you the truth, and just where you'll find them,
Get on to their track and keep close behind them.

Jim starts in the morning, says, to-day, I must work,
But when he gets to the "corners" he's seized with a jerk,
Of the mind and the will to the tavern to go,
(For he's too ill to work and he'll tell you so,)
And turning the corner marches on to the door,
Finds Tom, Dick and Harry, and of such a few more,
Who are all of a stripe, and who all jerked together,
With ailments alike for all seasons or weather.

Now Tom says to Jim, You're the last one come in,
It is your treat; come, bring in your gin:
But Jim says to Tom, I am strapt of a dime,
So you pay for it now, I will the next time.

But Tom says to Jim, I'm as poor off as Dick,
Who has been here before to-day and live upon trick.
But some how or other they all get a drink
Which make the eyes glimmer, you see by their wink.
All say, Mr. Landlord, let us have a cigar,
We see you have plenty of such things to spare.

Now keep a good lookout and you will discover
There is a fire at one end, and drunk fools at the other;
And to tell you the fact without any joke,
Their mouths are the chimneys that draw off the smoke,
And the longer they suck them, 'tis just as one s'poses,
Their cigars shorten up till they heat their red noses.
Having shortened their fuel to about an inch long,
They then are prepared for a chat or a song,
But before they commence they have an instinct,
They can do nothing right without more to drink.
From smoking they say they feel themselves thirsty,
From drinking again they feel themselves lusty;
And having secured more of the good creature,
Are now qualified to be each other's teacher;
And the feats of such loungers proves to us very clear
Where rum takes the lead the men have no fear.

Now each can tell over what feats he has done,
How wealth has poured in—how poor he begun.
In politics too they talk mighty brave,
Say the nation without them its union can't save,

They build mighty rail-roads, and ride the world over,
Get on at one end, and get off at the other,
Can tell what they saw in Paris or London,
And know all the streets in Moscow or Canton,
They helpt lay the telegraph under the ocean,
Turned the world upside down and set all in commotion,
Esteeming themselves the best of men,
Nothing great could be done without them.

But when you look on them and see their ill features,
You see only disgust wrapt up in such creatures,
And to speak the fact, they're a mean breed of brothers,
Born out of due time, almost without mothers,
And wherever they go they hatch up a muss,
And wherever they stay they're a curse.
Their influence is evil on the young and the old,
And the mischief they do can hardly be told,
And to sum up the matter and give no abuse,
Unless they reform they will generate nuisance.
If you follow their track and keep close behind them,
About as I have stated, I think you can find them.

And now please to pardon the pioneer digression;
For the good of our country I have given expression
That those who come after, bad example may shun,
And be saved from disgrace, or the ruin of rum.

THE PAST.

The few roads were then muddy, rough and crooked,
Used seldom by teams, but frequently footed,
Our swales and our swamps with cross-logs were laid,
With chinking between covered with dirt by a spade.
We wound up the hills by blazes on trees,
As best we could and with the most ease.
'Twas sometimes with horses, but often with oxen,
Our necessaries hauled, our carriages broken.
And sometimes endangered by the swelling flood,
Or the team and the axle would wallow in mud,
And thus pressing team with toil all the day
From five to ten miles advanced on our way.

Our mail matters then were placed in a sack,
And laid on a man to lug on his back.
And to pick his way lest you would think by his track,
Went this way and that way, like a horse that did rack.
Our four horse teams, then, if they hauled a ton,
Thro' the rough road and mud 'twas tho't had well done.
Then in a log stable, straw and provender before them,
For feed and for rest their strength to restore them,
Then for their drink used the cool running water,
Or through ice cut a hole to dip in their snorter.
Their harness was then made of leather to the tug,
Which would glisten like oil made out of mud.
Their bodies composed of bone, flesh, and skin,

Fit subjects for swarms of flies their blood to drain.

Our meadows were mown by scythe and rough snath,
Our boys then spread grass with a fork or a staff.
When our hay became dry, and some signs of a shower,
Then boys, girls, and mothers raked by the hour.
Our harvest then gathered with sickle in hand,
One clip at a time till none was left to stand.
And other things then worked after such a fashion,
Toil hard, was the word, but don't get in a passion.

THE PAST—THE PRESENT.

And now, fellow mortals, by way of reflection,
Let our minds run back to past recollection,
When the wilderness flourished unbroken by man,
When owls sang by night, and wild beasts freely ran,
When the Red man roamed o'er hill, vale and plain,
With his weapon in hand, in quest of wild game;
When the sound of the gospel had not reached his ear,
When civilization was far in the rear,
When the ox or the cow had not served their part,
In giving man food or in drawing the cart.
No genius to sweep off the wilderness waste,
To form fruitful fields, or supply in its place
The vine and the fruit tree, the flocks and the herds;
No cities with presses to issue forth words,

BRUNSWICK.

To spread forth the news and enlighten the minds,
But the savage in darkness dwelt here in those times.

Wise men from the East soon sought out the way
To the Star of the West to carry their sway,
In the arts and in science of civilized life,
Expelling the darkness of wildness and strife.
With much toil and hardship o'er a long, rough road
They sought out their way to make their abode,
Where the wild beasts and savages together run wild,
And the church bell and Sabbath never had smiled.

Now in came the Gospel refulgent with light,
To chase out the darkness and bring to their sight,
The endearments resulting from civilization,
And plant in the wild a God-fearing nation.
Their God is their trust; as saints they adore him.
The wilderness falls and the fields rise before them
The promising harvests tossed by breezes do wave,
All the wants are supplied that the appetite crave.
Our flocks and our herds our hills they adorn,
While our valleys still yield an abundance of corn.
The schools, academies and colleges combined,
Give proper instruction and expand the mind.
Our churches are reared with spires pointing to heaven
From which learned pastors pour fourth gospel leaven,
Which raises dull minds from low grounds of sadness,
To those fairer climes in the high plains of gladness,

BRUNSWICK.

Where may we all anchor in that haven of rest,
Prepared to meet God and dwell with the blest.

THE PRESENT.

Our roads are now graded, blazed trees have retired,
Our forests have faded and our swamps have dried.
We now pass in safety over permanent bridges,
And our valleys are passed by grading the ridges.
Our teamsters now travel full three times the distance,
With three times the load, with far less resistance.
And now in our meadows we'll just take a peep,
And see the man ride his scythe, perhaps half asleep.
But look how the grass falls all perfectly spread,
Ten acres each day he lays prostrate 'tis said.
But once do look, there is no mistake,
You see the man lazily riding his rake;
And yet, slowly riding, his hay comes together.
All these we now do without lifting a feather.
Another thing now-a-days, the fools it may tickle,
For the lazy old scamp is now riding his sickle,
And by the exertion of merely a motion,
See grain cut and gathered and laid to his notion.
Should inventions improve as we're inclined to be led
We will soon use a machine to ride us to bed.
But one thing's desired, yet almost without hope,
That we have a machine to help us to get up.

BRUNSWICK STATISTICS, 1861.

PERSONAL PROPERTY.	Number.	Value.
Horses,	563	$24,392
Cattle,	1,740	21,205
Sheep,	5,320	8,077
Hogs,	485	1,850
Carriages,	275	6,531
Appertaining to Merchandise.		1,800
Appertaining to Manufactories,		2,053
Moneys and Credits,		18,967
Wheat, bushels,	6,456	6,456
Corn, "	49,581	14,895
Butter, pounds,	61,669	6,150
Cheese, "	54,420	3,800
Oats, Grass seeds, and Potatoes,		4,780
Products of Orchards and Gardens,		3,270
Yearly value of township,		$124,226

CHATHAM.

Although the county was organized in 1813, it is worthy of being observed that settlements did not commence in every township simultaneously. Mankind are not inclined to live remote from each other; on the contrary, those who were born and reared in the same region, generally seek after and associate together. And in peopling a new country the timidity and the friendship of the female sex for near neighbors often induces families to settle near each other.

Chatham township was organized Dec. 5, 1833. The first township officers were Nedabiah Cass, Joel Lyon, and Iram Packard, trustees. At the first election there were only eleven voters, to wit: Gaylord C. Warner, Joel Lyon, Nedabiah Cass, Moses Parsons, Barney Daniels, Amasa Packard, Ebenezar Shaw, Amos Utter, Iram Packard, Harvey Edwards and Thomas F. Palmer. Six of which in 1861, are yet residents in the township.

The first election for Justice of the Peace was in May, 1835. Orin Shaw and Thomas F. Palmer were opposing candidates. Mr. Shaw had one vote majority. Moses Parsons and Thomas F. Palmer contested that election. A trial of strength of influence was had a second time, which being illegal was set aside. A new election was ordered. Orin Shaw and Amasa Packard Jr., were the opposing candidates, and Shaw was elected by a majority of two votes. Politics was not known in the strife; other causes fired the friends of each to array themselves against each other.

CHATHAM.

The first school was taught in a private dwelling in the fall of 1833 by Verta Richards, since deceased. The pupils at that school were Lydia, Chloe, Eliza and Joseph Palmer. Celia, Emeline Richards, Catharine, Polly and Cornelia Packard, Mary, Orin and Alfred Shaw and Catharine Frazell.

VISITING PARTY.

A party of what might be called at that time young folks, made the necessary arrangements to visit their acquaintances in Harrisville. The day came and all congregated, dressed in the *then* best style to go in company. Two choice pair of oxen were yoked, sleds were filled with clean straw, quilts were spread to prevent straw-beards from sticking to their choice calico or flannel dresses, and they started off at a good ox-trot on their visit. At that date it was considered a great convenience to have an ox team in which to travel, and no female considered her fashionable dignity insulted by riding in an ox sled or wagon.

FIRST MARRIAGE.

The first couple married were Henry K. Joline and Eleanor Parsons, in 1820, and thirteen years prior to the organization of the township. A messenger traveled through to Sullivan, a distance of fourteen miles without any horse, and piloted Esquire Close through the woods to Chatham to tie the marriage knot. When Esq. Close started for Sullivan, he came to the sage conclusion to go the trail to Harrisville and from there by another trail to his home, rather than to venture fourteen miles travel through woods.

CHATHAM.

The first child born was Samuel H. Parsons.

Moses Parsons was the first settler, and made the first opening in the township in 1819, about one mile south of the center. He came from Massachusetts, died in Chatham in the month of October, 1843, aged 74 years.

CHURCHES.

The first Congregational Church was organized in April, 1834, under the Union Plan, and was attached to the Presbytery. The names of members at its organization were Barney Daniels and wife, Ebenzer Shaw and wife, Joel Lyon and wife, Amasa Packard and wife, Gideon Gardner and wife, Iram Packard and wife, Orin Shaw and wife, George, Phillip, and Jacob and Sarah Packard, making 18 members. In 1843 a division or schism got root and eventually divided the church into two separate organizations, one part advocating the Presbyterian plan, the other sustaining the Oberlin plan. During the excitement two church edifices respectable in appearance and well finished, were built, two preachers were hired a part or all the time. Efforts were used by each denomination to secure large attendance, a spirit of emulation rather than vital piety prevailed. The pockets of each were often depleted to pay the monetary matters. They continued thus struggling for fifteen years. In process of time the schisms were either healed or died out, and the two became united in 1858, and now compose a large and influential church. There is at the center a Methodist Episcopal Church respectable in numbers and in influence.

To show that liberality was practised among the first settlers, take the following instance. Henry K. Joline

CHATHAM. 57

was, for many months, unable to labor, owing to painful and severe sickness, and his situation became known to those residing in Harrisville township. Every night they furnished watchers until he was able to be carried to another place. They came with teams, took himself and family to Harrisville township and supported him while there free of charge, and when he was supposed fully restored to health they brought himself and family to their own residence. Such was the feeling and such the noble principles of benevolence that existed among the first settlers, and thank God the same trial of character is still exhibited by them, though traveling down to life's sunset.

CHATHAM STATISTICS.

PERSONAL PROPERTY.	Number.	Value.
Horses,	716	$23,335
Cattle,	1,838	20,015
Sheep,	6,150	10,292
Hogs,	767	2,372
Carriages and Wagons,	85	2,865
Merchandise,		3,500
Manufacturing,		600
Moneys and Credits,		40,257
Wheat, bushels,	8,179	8,179
Corn, "	28,951	7,233
Butter, pounds,	71,610	7,160
Cheese, "	26,175	1,575
Orchards and Garden Products,		12,650
Total of yearly value,		$150,033

If the wealth that yearly results from the crops of Oats, Grass-seeds, Potatoes, Hay, and other articles of trade and commerce, were added, it would not be exceeding probability to place the annual products at $209.000.

Chatham is an agricultural township. Of course the fund invested in merchandise is limited in amount. The farmers, residing within fifteen miles of rail-road stations, are accustomed to go there with their surplus produce.

Although the township is comparatively young, since organization, there are evident traits of industry. Houses, barns and other buildings intended for accommodation and comfort, give evidence of taste and neatness not excelled by townships that have been longer settled.

GUILFORD.

The township of Guilford is called No. 1, in the 14th range of the Western Reserve, and was owned by four original purchasers. Roger Newbury, of Windham, Connecticut, owned the south-east quarter, Justin Eley, of Springfield, Masschusetts, owned the south-west quarter, Enoch Perkins, of Hartford, Connecticut, owned the north-east quarter; and Elijah White, of Hudson, Connecticut, owned the north-west quarter.

The first settlement in the township was made in the year 1817, by Henry Hosmer, Chester Hosmer, Mary T. Hosmer, Shubal Porter, Abigal Porter, Lyman Munson and Moses Noble, who came from Southwick and Westfield in Massachusetts. All are now living in, or near tho same place where they severally settled, except Moses Noble, who died in 1831. In 1816 John Wilson and his brother David commenced chopping and making the first opening in the north-east quarter of the township. In the same year William Moore commenced making an opening in the north-west quarter about one mile east from Chippewa Creek and within the limits of the farm now occupied by Jesse Smith. John Wilson and David yet live on, and own the land where they first commenced. William Moore now resides in Westfield township and owns a farm there.

In February, 1817, Henry and Chester Hosmer, Shubal Porter and Lyman Munson built a log house on the south bank of Hubbard Creek, and they with Mary T. Hosmer and Abigail Porter moved their household goods into it, on the first day of March, 1817.

That house was within four rods of the house now known as Dowd's Hotel. In those days the now flourishing village of Seville was un-originated. The Indians at that time had a village there where they tarried when on hunting excursions, containing about ten wigwams. In that year, along the lowlands of Chippewa and Hubbard creeks, elk, deer, bears and wolves were numerous.

The two streams were filled with excellent fish. In the same year William Hosmer left Southwick in Massachusetts, and traveled alone, and after a tedious journey of forty-nine days on foot came to the cabin of his relatives in Guilford, and settled with them. During this year, 1818, the accession of inhabitants to this settlement was few. Philo French came and settled near Wilsons. Timothy Phelps made an opening near Wm. Moore, and the family of William Wolcott settled in the township. This year the county of Medina was created. Prior to this year all of this county, part of Lorain and a small part of Ashland county belonged to Portage. A road was opened from the county seat, south through Montville and Guilford, in the direction of Wooster, and log bridges made over the two creeks, within the present corporate limits of Seville. A road was laid out on the east line of the township, north and south. The first couple married were David Wilson and Abigail Porter being two of the first settlers. The first child born was William Walcott in 1819 who died at the age of five years.

In 1819 Jonas Stiles and William H. Bell became residents. Bell made his first opening east of the present residence of Moses Shaw. In this year James and John Crawford settled in the north-west quarter of the township, where now reside many of their descendants. During this year Henry Hosmer erected a

GUILFORD.

hewed log house, two stories high, near where he now resides. In its day, and in that neighborhood it was considered a model edifice, and contrasted wonderfully with the wigwams of the Indians, or even the first cabins that had been built three years prior. Chester Hosmer built a hewed log house into which he moved his father and himself. The same land is now owned by Eben Brigham. In that house Cyrus Chapman was married to Jerusha Hosmer. After marriage they settled in Harrisville township. Guilford township was organized this year with only voters sufficient to make the organization legal. Wm. H. Bell, Lyman Munson and John Wilson were the first Trustees, and Jonas Stiles, the first township clerk. The first ground plowed in the township was by Shubal Porter near the flowering mills, south of Seville. The first frame building was erected by Henry Hosmer, on the grounds now covered by "Dowd's Hotel." The first death in the township was a child of Lyman and Nancy Munson. On May 20, 1820 an election was held for a justice of the peace. Nine votes were polled and upon counting the ballots it was announced that John Crawford had one vote, Timothy Phelps had two votes and John Smith had six votes, and was declared elected. The following are the names of the voters at that election; John Smith, W. H. Bell, Timothy Phelps, Samuel Owen, John Crawford, William Wolcott, Jonas Stiles, Lyman Munson and John Wilson. In the same year, at the October election, thirteen votes were cast, which was the entire poll of the township. During this year a State Road was laid out from Wooster to Cleveland, which was laid on the same ground with the same road that had been cut out the previous year. It was afterwards known as and called the "Pike."

The first store in Guilford was opened by Chauncy

Barker. His stock was small and soon sold, when he left for Connecticut and there died.

The first school-house erected in the township was west of the State Road and opposite Moses Shaw's present residence. It was built cabin fashion, a chimney of clay and sticks at one end, the roof of clapboards kept on by weigh poles, a puncheon floor, no loft, a rickety door made of clapboards swung an creaking wood hinges, two small windows with greased paper for panes instead of glass. Miss Adaline Dothee taught the first summer school and John Bell taught the winter school of 1821 and 1822. In this first Guilford Seminary, James A. Bell (thereafter State Representative,) Josiah, William and James Crawford, Levi Nye, Jacob Bell, Amer and Jacob Moore were students. In 1822 that school house was burned down, and in 1823 a second quite similar in model and convenience was erected on the ground where the store of Caughey, Leland & Co., now stands. Intellectual light was poured out in that house by Emeline Forbs during the summer, and by Nathaneal Bell during the winter.

This year a death occurred that spread a gloom over those who then resided along Chippewa and Hubbard creeks. In the month of November, Elijah Porter started from the residence of his son, Shubal Porter, to the County Seat on necessary business relative to a go to pension he was then receiving from the United States. He went on foot to Daniel Wilson's, where he borrowed a horse and started for Medina. Late at night the horse came home alone. Mr. Wilson and others soon were on their way, in the night, in the direction of Medina, searching for Mr. Porter. They found him about one and a half miles south of Medina setting at the root of a beach tree, so chilled that he could not speak. They attempted to carry him to the nearest house, which was at Medina, but before they got him there he died. His remains are interred in a graveyard west from David Wilson's residence, and it may be recorded that he was the first white man buried in Guilford township.

In the same year a Militia Company was organized, and to accomplish that object the whole of Harrisville, Westfield and half of Guilford townships had to be included in order that the necessary number of officers and soldiers could be got.

In 1824 the present burrying ground east of Seville was surveyed, and made by deed the property of the township for burial purposes. The first adult buried in that cemetery was Mrs. Harriet Wilson, wife of Robert Wilson. The same year Mrs. Margaret Wilson, wife of John Wilson, died and was buried west of David Wilson's, being the second person interred in that burying ground. During this year a school house was built at Wilson's Corners, being the third school house built in the township.

In 1825 a Mail Route was established between New Hampshire, in Huron county, and New Portage, in Portage county, and William Hosmer was the first appointed Post Master at Guilford Post Office.

Prior to the above date a Methodist society had been organized at Wilson's Corners, and David Wilson was the first class leader. Another Methodist society was, in 1826, started at the center of the township and Reuben Case was class leader. Circuit preachers came to those two places twice monthly and in course of a few years gathered together a number who are now exemplary christians of that denomination. This year (1826) a saw mill was erected and put in operation by Henry Hosmer and Nathaniel Bell.

In 1827 the settlers became patriotic and determined

to celebrate the 4th of July. An oration was delivered by Rufus Freeman, and a dinner of roast pigs, turkeys and chickens was prepared by David Clute.

In 1817, Guilford had made many advances in improvements and began to put forth united efforts to make use of the many natural advantages they discovered. The opening of roads from settlement to settlement converging at the Hosmer opening seemed to indicate that a town should be commenced, and in '28 Henry Hosmer, as proprietor, calling to his aid Nathaniel Bell, then county surveyor, surveyed and plotted a town to which was given the name of Seville, At that period Guilford could boast of two regular mail routs, an excellent tavern kept by Dr. Eastman, a school house, store, blacksmith shop, saw mill and a large number of industrious and experienced farmers, busily employed in cutting off the wilderness and opening for cultivation, beautiful and fertile farms. Not one boasted of being rich, but every one, under the guidance of a beneficent Providence, could say, " I have a competence and something to bestow."

NARRATIVE BY DAVID WILSON.

Myself and brother John first visited what is now called Guilford township in 1815, in April, and went west to Harrisville township. After tarrying there a short time we returned to Trumbull county. In the following December we came a second time, made a more thorough exploration, and returned unsatisfied. In 1819 we returned, purchased the north-east part of the township from Simon Perkins, then at Warren, and commenced making an improvement. Our house was built of bass-wood logs, measured 6 by 10 feet, roofed with the same kind of timber and chinked with moss. We chopped about two acres around our cabin and felt truly happy when seeing the noon-day sun shining through the openings on our dwellings. We often hunted and killed many deer. The choice pieces were salted down in a trough that we had scooped out; and after being in brine for some time were hung up and dried. Intending to go home to Warren a short time, we had hunted, killed, dressed and salted down a full trough of choice deer meat, intended for our use when we returned. In two months we came back, and upon examination found that the wild-cats had made openings into our house, carried off and devoured all of our salted deer meat. Nothing else was disturbed. Our beds were deer skins stretched between two poles, and the fat part of an arm was our pillow. Our table was one end of a broad puncheon that was run through an opening between the logs of our mansion. Our food was bear-meet, venison, wild turkey, potatoes, wild honey and tea made of spice wood. We had to go five miles through thick wood to get our pone bread baked, and we have often carried a bushel of potatoes that distance and complained not of the weight. Snakes were very numerous, but we did not dread them. My brother and I came among a den of rattlesnakes once when out hunting, and in a very short time we killed eighty, and could, if inclined, have killed more.

GUILFORD STATISTICS.

PERSONAL PROPERTY.	Number.	Value.
Horses,	675	$35,445
Cattle,	1,916	18,113
Sheep,	4,153	7,603
Hogs,	1,224	4,452
Carriages and Wagons,	301	10,743
Invested in Merchandising,		23,477
Invested in Manufacturing,		5,057
Moneys, Credits, Book Accounts,		86,398
Butter, pounds,	86,790	8,750
Cheese, "	14,625	878
Wheat, bushels,	20,416	20,400
Corn, "	79,790	19,945
Total of yearly value,		$241,261

If the value of oats, grass seeds, potatoes, wool and orchard products be computed and added to the above it will make the yearly value of the personal property and products of the township and village to exceed $315.000. In 1822, there were eighty-four cattle and ten horses listed by John Bell, valued at $1,072. To compare the list of property for taxation in 1819, with those of 1861, for the same purpose, shows an increase that few of former times ever expected to see or realize. The Wilsons, Hosmers and Porters can look back with pleasure upon the advances made since their first settlement in Guilford.

GRANGER.

ORGANIZATION.

The township was organized in February, 1820. A military company was raised and organized in 1819. John Burt was elected Captain, John Burt, Lieutenant and N. A. Goodwin, Ensign. At this date there were forty families in the township, amounting to about two hundred and sixty persons. The first township election was held at the house of Seth Paul, on the first Monday in April, 1820. The first township trustees were N. A. Goodwin, S. Paul and Festus Ganyard. John Codding was the first township clerk, Burt Codding was the first justice of the peace. For some time the people were without an elected constable. In January, 1822, the trustees met and appointed Ira Ingraham constable. The first money paid into the township treasury was twenty-five cents, being a fine imposed for swearing. Of that money, one half was paid out for paper on which to record township proceedings; the other half of the township fund was paid to William Paul for bringing the Laws and Journals from the county seat.

The first couple married were Stephen Woodward and Abigail Hill.

The Congregational Church was organized by Rev. W. Hanford and Caleb Pitkins in November 14, 1819, with the following church members: Elizar Hills, Abigail Hills, James Ganyard and Phebe Ganyard, Friend Ingraham and Lydia Ingraham, John Turner and Dolly

Turner, Lawrence Moore and Mary Moore, Wealthy Dyer, Charity and Hannah Turner — ten members.

The first Methodist Episcopal Class was formed in the autumn of 1820, by Elder Nunn, with the following members: Bela Spencer and Lydia Spencer, Alexander Spencer, Deborah Goodwin, Samuel Griffin, James Griffin, Jehial Porter and Hannah M'Cloud.

The first Baptist Church was formed in 1826, with the following members, by Elder Henry Hudson: Jesse H. Smith, Samuel Crosby and wife, David Holmes, Allen Smith and Phebe Grover.

From those small beginnings the same churches have now grown, and each exerts a salutary and christian influence among the present increasing inhabitants in Granger.

Could a roll be called in each church above named, how many of the first founders could answer personally? Head stones in grave yards can tell the resting place of many of them.

The first Physician who settled in Granger was Dr. Rufus Pomroy, in the spring of 1829.

The first cabin built in the township was put up by Ezekiel Mott, in the spring of 1816, on Lot 2, being the land now owned by George M. Codding.

The first male born in the township was Hamilton Low, son of Hiram. The first female born was Deborah Goodwin. The two aforesaid first births were August 2, 1818.

The first school in the township was kept by William Paul, on lot 42, in the winter of 1819 and 1820, and numbered seventeen scholars, among whom were John M. Ganyard, John M'Farlen and others.

The first law suit was between Seymour W. Green and Anthony Low. Mr. Seymour's cow lost, from her neck, a bell. Some months thereafter, Mr. Low found

a bell; Seymour said it was his, Low thought it very
doubtful; suit was brought, parties appeared, statements
without anger, were made. The justice awarded the
bell to Seymour, and made him pay the costs, as he
gained the suit.

JAMES GANYARD.

James Ganyard was born January 14, 1772, at Killingsworth, and Phebe, his wife, was born at Saybrook,
1768. They left Connecticut, their native State, and
came to Bristol, Ontario county, New York, in 1793.
At that date the place where they settled was considered the extreme border of civilization and was then
called Phelps and Gorham's purchase.

In the month of October, 1815, Mr. Ganyard, in
company with Eleazer Hills, Anthony Low and Burt
Codding, came to Ohio to view No. 3, Range 13 of the
Western Reserve and to purchase, if they were satisfied
with location and price. After viewing land and advantages, they returned and purchased of Gideon Granger, who was the proprietor of three-fourths of the
township, at four dollars per acre. They sold their
farms in Bristol to Mr. Granger in part payment, and
for the balance yet due to him, gave mortgage upon
their new purchase. That mortgage proved a serious
hinderance to the settlers in Granger township for many
years thereafter. After the agreement was made, and
before the written contract was signed, Mr. Ganyard
transferred his right of proprietorship to Mr. John
Codding, reserving only to himself so much land as he
had paid for. This is why his name never appeared
on the written record of the company. Mr. Ganyard
settled on lot 15, in Granger, in 1811, being the same

farm on which his son J. N. Ganyard resided in 1860. Mr. James Ganyard died of dropsy, December 20, 1844. Mrs. Phebe Ganyard died of inflammation of the brain, March 2, 1840. Their remains occupy graves in the burial ground on the same farm, one-half mile north from Grangerburg. A humble stone bearing their names is now the only memorial that remains to tell of two who were among the first settlers in Granger.

ANTHONY LOW.

Anthony Low was born in Providence, Rhode Island, in 1766, and in due time of life claimed, by apprenticeship, the appellation of carpenter and joiner. He went to Wyoming, when a young man, with the intention of carrying on his trade, and while there formed an acquaintance with Mary Baldwin, to whom he was afterwards married. She was born in Pennsylvania, in 1772, and was when young, taken prisoner by the Indians. Though young, she witnessed many of the bloody scenes and murders perpetrated by the Indians who then roamed wild masters on either side of the Susquehannah river. Over her own head was brandished the bloody tomahawk of the reckless wild man. She witnessed the taking of infants from mothers by the heels, and their brains dashed out by being thrown against a log or tree, and their bodies left upon the ground to molder and rot. She has witnessed the wife forced to sit in mute silence while the scalp was being rudely cut from the head of the fond husband, and then witnessed the tomahawk buried in his head. She has, when a prisoner, witnessed the burning of the dwellings of the whites, and while the flame was curling upward, heard the sad cries of the inmates whose doom was then either to be burned, or to be slain by those who surrounded the burning dwellings. Mr. Baldwin, the father of Mary, had eight sons—all of them large and strong men. Three were colonels and acted conspicuously during the Indian wars of those days. The house of Mr. Baldwin was set on fire twice by the Indians. A third effort was being made, when one of the sons discovered an Indian near the dwelling upon whom he sprang quickly and fearlessly and killed him by planting a hatchet in his forehead.

Anthony Low died in November, 1824 aged 58, and his wife, Mary Low, in August, 1838 aged 66. They were buried on lot 2, in Granger.

Jesse Perkins, a worthy young man, came into the township in 1818, was taken sick when living at the house of Mr. John Turner, then in Copley, where he died, April 8, 1819. His remains were brought to Granger and interred in lot 5, and his was the first grave in the township.

All of the foregoing are collected from a written manuscript that can be seen at the residence of Festus Ganyard, a son of Mr. James Ganyard, who has lived to a good old age and witnessed the great and profitable changes that have taken place in Granger township since 1817.

The following history and incidents are from the manuscripts of Mr. W. Cogswell. He begins with the history of his ancestors dating back about two centuries.

William Cogswell, the great-great-grandfather of the narrator, was born in Ipswich, England, sixty-two miles north-east from London. He was well educated in navigation, and became the owner of a vessel in 1666, and taking in a company, sailed for America, landing at Boston Harbor. While there he accompanied a portion of those he had brought over, in quest of a location, which when selected, was named Ipswich, after his native place and the name of his vessel. After making several voyages to and from England, he finally settled in Ipswich, America. Edward, his son, was born April 17, 1685, and died April 17, 1773. Samuel, son of Edward, was born March 1, 1710, and died April 11, 1775. William, son of Samuel, and father of the present William Cogswell, was born November 2, 1748, and died in Granger township, May 12, 1838. Although he was deprived of a regular education, he made mathematics his choice study, and by continued application in that branch, became famous as an almanac compiler in early life. When near life's close he gave directions as to his burial, requesting Jehial Porter to preach his funeral sermon from the text "Blessed are they that die in the Lord;" selected the hymn that he wished to be sung, and uttered the following words: "I am nearly eighty years old, was never at fifty cents' expense for a doctor bill, never lost, by sickness, a meal in sixty years, but lost a great many meals on account of having nothing to eat."

My mother was a daughter of Lieutenant Gates, who served during the Revolutionary war. She was born in Canterbery, Connecticut, in 1772, and during life, passed through many trying scenes and privations. Among these scenes was the bloody massacre of Wyoming, of which she was one of the survivors. She there witnessed the savage spectacle of sacrificing prisoners at the stake. One poor fellow had his body and limbs filled with dry splinters, then fastened to a tree and burned to death. Another had a portion of his bowels, when cut out, fastened to a sapling and himself forced to walk around that sapling until all his bowels came out, when he fell dead. The old woman saw the Indian approaching, brandishing his bloody tomahawk, and she attempted to divert him from his bloody purpose by kindly offering him some bread and beef. The offer had the desired effect. The savage asked where her papooses (children) were; she pointed to each one of them, and was ordered by the cruel savage to take them to a certain corner in the fort and sit down. She did so, and while there thanked God for her deliverance, and of those with her, and she devoutly prayed that God would be a protector to her and to the children. That prayer was heard and answered. She lived long and happily after witnessing that cruel massacre, and died in Bath, at the age of seventy-seven, and is there buried. Four of the survivors who witnessed the Wyoming massacre, after being long separated during life, are buried within four miles of each other in Bath and Granger.

WILLIAM COGSWELL'S HISTORY.

I was born February 20, 1794, at the Great Bend of the Susquehanna, N. Y. In 1797, my father, William, sold, and removed from New York to Alleghany county, Pennsylvania, near Redstone Old Fort. In 1801, he became the owner of two hundred acres of land in Beaver county, Pennsylvania, by virtue of a soldier's right. In April, 1802, he moved there. Provisions were then scarce and costly. Often he was forced to leave home and work for means to supply his family. Once, when leaving, my mother made the inquiry with anxiety what should she do if provisions were exhausted before his return? I give his answer:" There is a half barrel of bran; sift it and make bread of it. When that is gone, go to the potatoe patch and dig out the old potatoes without disturbing the roots; boil them and use them with milk. When they are gone, follow the cows in the woods, see what herbs they eat, pick of the same, boil them and eat that with milk." Having gone forty miles, secured employment and got paid in corn, he joyfully returned with his hard earnings. A tree was cut down, a hole burned in the stump, a spring-pole erected, by means of which the corn was pounded and made ready for use, and in that way fed seven in the family.

When ten years old, I was in the absence of my father, compelled to chop and prepare fuel. I had no shoes to wear in the winter season. To keep my feet from freezing I heated a board at the fire, carried out, stood on it when chopping. When it became cold I brought it in, heated it, and in that way made it answer for shoes and stockings.

In progress of time, rights to land were often in dispute, and among the unlucky, it was discovered that my father had settled on the wrong piece. Though he had made an opening, erected his cabin and settled down, as he then supposed, for years, another Soldier's Right lawfully claimed the land, and he was forced to give up possession.

Becoming acquainted with Judge Oliver Phelps, then the owner of Granger township, my father visited that township in 1807 and found it wholly unsettled. Being pleased with appearances of soil, timber and its other natural advantages, he made a selection of three hundred and seventy acres, now comprised in the three lots owned by Isaac Low, C. R. Spencer and Job Green. He went from Granger to Warren, Trumbull county, and contracted with Calvin Austin, agent of Phelps, for the land, and paid the sum required. Some time thereafter Phelps became insolvent, his title to lands seized by creditors and sold. My father having purchased on contract, was forced to loose what he had paid, and was again prevented from being a land holder. He resided in Beaver county until 1815, when he removed to Columbiana county, Ohio. In 1818 he again came to Granger, bought by article the lot now owned by Job Green, and settled thereon, and for six years struggled through the many hardships incident to first settlers. About the time his article expired he found himself unable to make payment, owing to want of price for produce. He sold his claim to his sons William, Samuel and Nathaniel, who continued to reside there and make improvements. In 1824 I became, by purchase, sole owner, concluded to select another locality, sold my right to land in Granger township and moved into Bath township, Summit county, where I now (1861) reside.

I must now make a break in my history, otherwise the pioneer community will cast me out of the synagogue. In 1810, in company with my uncle Gibson Gates and Hezekiah Burdick (two of the first settlers in Bath) I left the home of my father, traveled by way of Vannatt's Ford on the Mahoning river to the house of Gates in Bath. I remained there until August of that year, when, in company with Gates and John Manning, I started for Granger township. Our road (old settlers called it course) was through Richfield by way of L. May (now widow Biglow's land,) thence westwardly to Panther Cave in Hinckley. We visited that cave in search of game, but saw no panthers. From thence we traveled to where an Indian gallows was standing in the big bend of the Rocky River. In 1806, a squaw had been hung there, charged with witchcraft. The squaw had said that there would be darkness on the face of the earth in June, which the ignorant Indians decided to be undoubted proof of witchery. She was hung in May, and on the 13th of June, 1806, there was an eclipse of the sun. After viewing the gallows, we traveled on southerly, and at night encamped under a ledge of rocks near where Isaac Low now resides, about thirty rods from the last named place. I at that time, carved the initials of my name on a beach tree which can be seen to this day. After feasting on wild turkey, for breakfast, we pursued our course and came on to the "Smith Road," about where the Squaw Tavern now stands. This was my first visit into and through Granger. It was then truly a wilderness; the marks of the pioneers were few. When my rememberance brings to mental view those times and contrast the changes, I am astonished, and must say that greater improvements are now seen than the most sagacious then anticipated.

In January, 1813, the War Department found it necessary to build three small gun boats to be used in annoying the larger vessels of the enemy. It was soon discovered by Captain Perry that small vessels, being more easily and rapidly managed, could do effective service in close contest. The contract for building the boats was awarded to Brimel Robins, of Alleghany Co., Pennsylvania, who selected "Old Portage," on the Cuyahoga River, as the place where to build them. The timber and lumber were furnished by Captains Rice and Stowe and sawed in the mill of Francis and Zenas Kelsey, at "old Cuyahoga village." Stewart Gaylord superintended the then boat yard. In June the three gun boats were launched, and dubbed with the names of "Tripp, Tigress and Portage." I was employed with others, to float them down to the Lake, with instructions that when we got to the "Pinery," we should furnish each boat with mast and spars.

While floating downward toward our destination a tree was descried that had fallen into the stream and must, unless removed, stop the boats. Being then young and full of life, I attacked the log with axe, and when nearly ready to float, I lost my balance, falling into water about fifteen feet in depth. After sounding, I made vigorous efforts and came to surface with axe in hand, and swam to the shore. I name this occurrence, not as a feat, but to say how very difficult it is to rise to the surface or to swim when one limb of the body is heavier than the other.

At the Pinery we were detained several days in procuring the necessary rigging for the boats. At that place I killed a porcupine, which was looked upon as an animal of great curiosity by our small crew. When we got to Cleveland the gun-boats were examined by many and the general opinion was that they were the kind needed. When at Cleveland I became very patriotic and wished to enlist under Captain Perry, but decided to go home first, and after making proper arrangements, to return and become a soldier. My mother, having tested in part the scenes and privations of the Revolutionary war, seemed opposed to my enlisting, and by rehearsals of incidents which she had witnessed, dampened my ardor, and I finally consented to remain a private, and not brave the storms of Lake Erie in a small gun boat.

In the summer of 1814, I was employed by Messrs. Warner and Coit to make salt at the Liverpool salt springs, where I continued until the following December. I not only labored at making salt, but was compelled to keep watch against the Indians who at that time roamed much and often in Columbia and Liverpool neighborhoods and kept the few white inhabitants in fear. The price of a bushel of Liverpool salt was $5.

When winter fairly set in, I started for Granger in company with Dan Mallet, intending to make hunting our main business for some weeks. For some time we killed ma●●●all game. After some days we found a long-legged bear in an alder swamp. When he discovered us he commenced a retreat. As he passed near me I fired, but without effect. The two dogs next attacked him, which he siezed, and commenced hugging and biting them. I reloaded and fired a second time, the ball disabling his fore-leg, when he immediately let go of the dogs and commenced biting his maimed limb. After venting his spleen upon the maimed limb, in despite of dogs, he came toward me in a very menacing manner. I retreated rapidly, but reloaded as I ran, and when fully prepared wheeled about and fired. The ball took lodgment in the mad bruins jaw, causing it to hang downward. At this juncture, Mallett came up to the chase from the opposite side of the swamp, and taking deliberate aim lodged a ball in the brain of the bear and ended the contest and the race. The next day we procured an old horse, on which we carried to Liverpool the game we had shot during our hunting excursion. In those days an axe and rifle constituted my chattel property, and it then seemed to me that I had all that was necessary.

After staying at Liverpool some time to complete a chopping contract, I again started for the residence of my uncle Gates, near the Cuyahoga. At this early date there were no lot lines in Brunswick or Hinckley; therefore I traveled a course by guess. I had got into the N. W. part of Bath when night came on. Wearied and hungry I halted, struck up a fire, peeled some bark with which to make a bed, arranged it in hunter's style and drawing my slouch hat over my face, fell into a pleasant sleep, and remained unmolested until morning. When I awoke in the morning I found my bark coverlet beautifully adorned with a covering of snow about three inches in depth. I arose early, and left my bed for the accommodation of any who might need it. I had designed to reach the cabin of Mr. E. Hale, when I left Liverpool; still I was not there. On my way, in the morning, to Mr. Hale's, I killed two deer. Upon arriving at Mr. Hale's, I informed her that I stood in much need of dinner, supper, breakfast and dinner, having eaten nothing since I left Liverpool. Mrs. Hale informed me that she had some hominy that she would warm for me. I told her to set it on the table and I would warm it by eating. She did so, and I fared sumptuously and thankfully on cold hominy. In traveling from the cabin of Elijah to Jonathan Hale's, I killed a noble buck, which I sold to Jonathan for two dollars. After remaining a short time, I again commenced rambling from place to place in quest of work or game.

In 1815, I had an interview with a bear, that to this day causes me to shudder when I think of the hazardous adventure. I. Sippy, D. Willey, Wm. Ben and myself were felling a tree for coons, when the barking of our three dogs, at a distance, admonished us that they had found game. When we came to the dogs, we discovered that they were in close combat with a bear, in the hollow of a large tree that was fallen. I crawled in the length of my body, caught the hind legs of two dogs and succeeded in dragging them out. I then crawled in a second time, got hold of the leg of the remaining dog and by hard pulling succeeded in rescuing him from the tight hug of the bear. The dog died soon after being brought out. Soon thereafter the enraged bear showed his head at the opening, when a blow from an axe, given by Sippy, nearly severed the snout from the head. The bear drew back, but in a very few minutes, again poked out his mutilated head for which Sippy had been anxiously watching. A second stroke burried the axe in the head of bruin, who ceased to draw back. We drew him out and estimated his weight, when dressed, at four hundred pounds. That encounter often makes me think of Putman and the wolf.

During this hunting excursion we killed twenty-nine raccoons, one woolly nig and the before mentioned bruin.

In 1816, in company with Sippy, I roamed over portions of Granger, Bath and Hinckley, in order to get up a supply of honey, hops and cranberries on which to trade. During our wanderings from place to place, we often shot wild game and occasionally a bear. In the fall of the year, the bears were accustomed to visit wild groves where acorns or chestnuts grew, and very often a bullet from the well aimed rifle of the hunter caused bruin to fall from an oak or chestnut tree, on which he had perched himself to feed upon his favorite food.

In 1818, I became a permanent citizen of Granger, after having often roamed alone, and sometimes in company with others, over the territory now comprised in the townships of Liverpool, Brunswick, Medina, Granger, Hinckley, Bath and Copley, in quest of game or in search of trade or employment. My brother-in-law, Sippy and myself, purchased by article the land where C. R. Spencer now lives, on which we paid one hundred and sixty dollars. That summer we cleared and planted six acres of corn and a large patch with potatoes. In the fall of that year, I visited the home of my father, and after a short stay he and family removed with me to Granger. My father, Sippy and myself cut the first opened road from Cuyahoga to Granger, at our own expense; and while thus employed we camped out many nights, and our only vegetable food was potatoes roasted and eaten with the meat of wild game that we occasionally shot. I have assisted at the raisings of the first cabins in Richfield, Bath, Copley, Sharon, Granger, Hinckley, Brunswick and Liverpool townships. I have often walked eight or ten miles in company with others, to assist in raising a house or barn, and when done considered it no hardship to walk home in the evening, and not unfrequently after night, lighted by burning torches of hickory bark. To ride through the woods in 1818, was no easy or pleasant task.

When Sippy and myself articled for the land referred to, we were to have one hundred and forty acres at five dollars per acre. At the close of four years we had what was then considered tolerably good cabins put up, had cleared about forty acres, and were beginning to have some of nature's wildness tamed, when our article run out, and we were unable to pay as stipulated. Wheat was then twenty-five cents per bushel and other kinds of trade equally low. Trade was then, like the man who had a dog which he sold for one dollar, and gave the same for two pups, at fifty cents each. Stringency in money forced us to give up our right to the land. We lost all we paid, all our labor and improvements and had to start out anew, in search of homes that we wished to be permanent.

I will narrate one more incident, and in so doing, I have no wish to seem egotistical, nor yet possessed of more than ordinary courage.

Having lost some of our cattle, Sippy and myself concluded to make search for them. While rambling in the woods, the bark of the old dog gave notice that he had found some kind of game. When we came to the spot we descried an animal perched high in a tree, that looked to be of the panther tribe. We had no guns with us, and to dislodge the animal, we must have recource to a different mode of warfare. Upon a nearer approach, we discovered our supposed panther to be a wild cat of no common size. I proposed to climb the tree, and shake the animal off; but was reminded by Sippy that "pussey's" claws were not easily displaced by violent limb shaking. Determined to make battle, I cut a club of proper heft, and ascended the tree. When within ten feet of the limb on which pussy squatted, I stopped to take a look at the critter. The green glaring eyes made me feel uncomfortable, but my position indicated that I should be courageous. With left hand, I took firm hold of a limb, with my right hand I wielded the bludgeon. As I stood watching, pussy made, first, a few quick shakes of the short tail, and instantly bounded down towards my face. Instantly I parried off its descent with the club, and sent the animal rapidly to the ground. The dog was on hand, and made jaw-love to "pussy." A hard fight of scratching and biting ensued, which was terminated by Sippy giving pussy a blow (lucky or unlucky) that terminated that critter's existence. I frankly acknowledge that the menacing of that cat made me feel rather unpleasant when on the tree, and I consider the risk of killing it more hazardous than when in a hallow tree, trying to extricate my dogs from the hug of the bear.

On July 8, 1820, the sparsely settled citizens of Granger had met, by invitation, to raise a barn on the farm now occupied by David Sheldon. Lyman Isbel was there aiding. A log forty feet long was in progress of being pushed on to the building. By want of necessary care, one end of the log got from the pikes used in pushing, causing the other end to be displaced and the log rolled from the building upon the body of Mr. Isbell, killing him instantly. The body was placed on a sled and hauled to his home. Late in the evening I was requested to go to the residence of Dr. Henry Hudson, in the north-east part of Bath and get him to preach the funeral sermon, at the house of Mr. Isbell the following day at 11 A. M.

I started on foot and got to the house of Mr. Hale, (where the preacher boarded,) after dark, but found no preacher. Mr. Hale informed me that he was (as he supposed) at Cuyahoga Falls. I went there, and was informed that he had gone to Fish Creek to preach that evening. To Fish Creek I traveled, where I found him at three o'clock in the morning. We then prepared to return to Granger by way of Cuyahoga Falls, and reached the house of the deceased in time to meet the appointment.

I name the sudden death of Mr. Isbell because he was a worthy man, and I give a statement of the journey after a preacher, to apprise young men of the present day that a trip of thirty miles, *on foot in the night, and through the woods* was undertaken and accomplished with less complaint, in 1820, than a young man will now make after walking, in the day time, five miles.

BEAR HUNT.—During the early settlement there was a she bear, who annoyed the settlers by frequently carrying off (without leave,) hogs, calves and other domestic animals. She was often threatened, and as often pursued. In the winter of 1822, I was hunting in the north-west part of Granger, when I came on her trail, which was known to all hunters, by the unusual length of the strides. She was escorted by two cubs. I called on Sippy and told him of my discovery and proposed that we should go in search, and if possible, bring the lady to terms. The next morning we were early on the trail, intending if possible, to rid the neighborhood of the "old pest." We followed the trail all day through Hinckley, and toward evening, discovered dead bees on the snow. We soon found the tree, which we chopped down and found more than one hundred pounds of beautiful honey. We scooped out a trough with the axe and filled it with choice honey-comb; and night coming on we encamped there, faring sumptuously on bread, (which we carried with us) and honey. Next morning we breakfasted early on honey and bread, and pursued the trail. After pursuing the zigzag tracks for some miles, we came to a large basswood, in which was the bear and her two cubs. Marks about the tree seemed to say that it had been tenanted by the old depredator for years. We concluded we had the "old gal" in close quarters, and commenced by sturdy blows to fell the tree. The tree fell slowly, being impeded by limbs of other trees, of which occurence the bear took advantage and made a leap from the tree before it struck the ground. We supposed the "old sinner" would, at least, tarry till the tree fell, but she was off at bear speed. I fired, but the ball took no effect. Sippy soon dispatched the two cubs with his axe. The next day, with horses and sled we hauled home cubs and honey.

SAME OLD BEAR.—In October, 1623, I was hunting in the north part of Granger, and I had killed two turkeys and a deer; and after traveling about a mile from where I had hung them up, I came across the identical thieving, old " she bear." She seemed as though she knew me, but did not tarry long. I raised my gun and fired; the ball lodged in her hip. As I pursued, I reloaded and fired a second time, and broke a fore leg. When the leg was broke the bear stopped, sat up and bit the maimed limb, and then was off at full speed. I started in pursuit, from where John Truman now lives, through the south-west part of Hinckley, then into Brunswick, then across Plumb Creek, then down the creek, then east into Hinckley, and lastly into an alder swamp near where Earl Salsbury now lives. She secreted in the mud and water of that swamp, keeping her head up. I went within proper distance, fired, and killed her, and thus terminated her swinish propensities. The chase of that bear, was about the sweatiest, longest and hardest race I ever ran. The death of that " old huzzy " gained to me the plaudits of many whose sheep, hogs and calves had been taken and devoured by that same thievish bear.

CONTRACT FOR LAND.—In 1824, my father finding himself unable to pay for his farm, according to the stipulations of his article, proposed that I should go to Mr. Seymour's, who lived in Canandaigua, N. Y., and get the same land articled to myself and brothers. I consented traveled to Cleveland, from thence, by schooner to Buffalo, and thence to Canandaigua. Mr. Seymoor heard my statement and consented to release the State's claim upon the two lots which Aaron Spencer had bought, provided Spencer would buy the lot on which my father was settled and then article it to me and my brothers, which was afterwards done.

I have now given a few of the incidents of my Pioneer life ; and when I look back where I was, what I have encountered and endured, I seem astonished to think that I yet live. An over-ruling Providence watched over and graciously guided. And in 1861, I look upon and roam over hills and valleys, once vocal with the yell of the red man, and the many wild sounds of the beasts of the forest. I have lived to see a wilderness blossoming and budding. I have lived to see a younger generation happily enjoying the rich boons resulting from their fathers' toil, and in my years of decline I not only wish them present comfort and happiness, but a full share of all that kind Providence may in future bestow.

GRANGER STATISTICS.

PERSONAL PROPERTY.	Number.	Value.
Horses,	470	$24,776
Cattle,	1,503	19,518
Mules,	2	80
Sheep,	8,141	14,586
Hogs,	429	1,431
Carriages and Wagons,	175	5,670
Merchandise,		3,300
Manufacturing,		1,400
Moneys, Credits,		40,560
Butter, pounds,	7,757	7,757
Cheese, "	27,965	6,991
Wheat, bushels,	54,625	5,462
Corn. "	17,200	1,032
Total of yearly value.		$132,575

To these may be added the yearly value accruing from Oats, Grass-seeds, Potatoes, Fruits of Orchards and Gardens, - - - - - - - 21,756

Total estimate, - - - - - $154,325

If the products made and sold by families, eggs, rags, and all other articles of trade or commerce were strictly counted, the yearly personal value of the township would exceed $175,000.

Industry produced it—economy saved it.

HARRISVILLE.

The following narrative of the first settlements made in the township of Harrisville was compiled by Dr. E. H. Sibley, who had made it a point of interest and duty to call personally on Joseph Harris and other old pioneers and learn from them the perils and privations consequent upon first settlements. Though collected and compiled in November, 1858, it may be truly styled pioneer history. Some of the actors then named are since deceased.

INCIDENTS

Relating to the Early History and Settlement of Harrisville township, Medina county, in the State of Ohio, being No. 1 in the 19th Range of Townships of the Western Reserve.

In 1807 the Connecticut Company made a division of their lands west of the Cuyahoga River Township. Number One in the Sixteenth Range (Harrisville,) was drawn by sixteen corporates, viz: Nehemiah Gaylord, John and Jabes Gillett, Sol. Rockwell and brothers, Hezekiah Huntington, William Battell, Russel Burr, Job Curtis' heirs, Thomas Huntington, Royal Tylee, Wright and Sutliff, Joseph Haines, Martin Kellogg, Burr and Loomis, Joseph Battell, and Eliphalet Austin, known by the name of the Torringford Company--together with two thousand acres in township number One, the Fifteenth Range, to compensate for the swamp land in Harrisville township. In 1810, the township was surveyed into lots of one hundred acres each, and a road was, during the year, established by the Company of Portage county, through the number One, from the Franklinton road in Norton, west through the center to the east line of Huron county. The Legislature also, during this year, established a State road from Mansfield to Cleveland, through the township, and appropriated eight hundred dollars toward opening the same. It was during this year that the Torringford Company made a subdivision of their land in Harrisville, and made Joseph Harris their agent to effect sales. The price was established at two dollars per acre, Mr. Harris having the privilege of selecting two hundred acres as a pioneer settlement location, to be deducted from his undivided portion. It was in this year, viz: In 1810, that Mr. Harris made his selection and built his house. On February 14, 1811, Mr. Harris moved his family into Harrisville, consisting of himself, wife and one child then about two years old, together with James S. Redfield, then a lad about eleven years old.

Their nearest neighbors were at Wooster, seventeen miles south on the Killbuck river. The location selected by Mr. Harris, had been the favorite hunting grounds of the Wyandot and Ottawa Indians, and many of their wigwams were standing near the spot he selected for the site of his present residence—and in a good state of preservation. While once making excavations for his cellar, many of the bones of their ancestors were found. Still, although the social relations that subsisted at this time between Mr. Harris and these denizens of the forest, were of the most friendly and reciprocal character, yet true to their national characteristics they preferred retirement from the proximity of the pale faces, abandoning their lodges, and

building new ones from two to six miles distant. In
June of this year, Mr. George Burr and his wife in
company with Russell Burr, came out from Litchfield
county, Connecticut, and settled on the lot adjoining
Mr. Harris, and in the following September, the Messrs.
Calvin and Lyman Corbin, from the city of Boston,
Massachusetts, purchased and settled on the farm now
owned by George Burr. No important event occurred
in the settlement from this on until about the first day
of July, 1812, when a messenger arrived from Randolph, in Portage county, bringing a newspaper
containing the declaration of war, also a letter warning
the settlers of their danger, as it was not then known
in whose interest the Indians would enlist, and urgently
soliciting them to return to the older settlements. A
consultation was held in the evening, which resulted
in the conclusion that under existing circumstances it
would be safer to repair to the settlements until something more decisive could be learned in relation to our
affairs on the then extreme north-western frontier.
Accordingly the next morning Mr. Harris, Russell and
George Burr, with the Corbins, loaded their most
valuable furniture and household goods on wagons,
and with seven yoke of oxen, started for Randolph,
George Burr's wife having gone there some weeks
previous. Almost at the outset, unfortunately one of
the wagons was overturned, throwing Mrs. Harris and
the child from the wagon—but quite undaunted, although badly bruised, she insisted on going forward,
and that the journey might be expedited she was
mounted with her child on the only horse in the settlement, and accompanied by her husband on foot reached
their friends in Randolph the next morning, having
been obliged to lie out over night in the woods, on
account of having lost the trail when within a mile or

two of the settlement. The settlers in leaving their homes, of necessity had to abandon their crops, and as the prosperity of the settlement depended on their being secured, Mr. Harris, on the following Monday morning mounted his horse, shouldered his trusty rifle and accompanied only by his faithful dog, wended his solitary way back to Harrisville. As he approached the settlement, he discovered that some persons had been in the vicinity during his absence. On examining the track, he discovered that some had been made with shoes and some with moccasins. Dismounting his horse and muffling the bell (an appendage by the way which all the early settlers were in the habit of attaching to their "Equine" domestics,) he silently and cautiously proceeded to examine the Indian trail leading from Sandusky to the Tuscarawas, and no appearances of Indians having passed along it, he soon came to the conclusion that some white person must have been in the vicinity during his absence.

On entering his cabin, appearances indicated that a number of persons had passed a night there, having used some of his iron ware for the purpose of cooking. It was afterwards ascertained that the Commissioners who were appointed by the legislature to establish a road from Mansfield to Cleveland, passed a night at Mr. Harris's house cooking their supper and breakfast there. Mr. Harris finding that his wheat was not yet fit for harvesting, set about hoeing out his corn and potatoes. After having been here about ten days, Russell Burr and Elisha Sears came out and harvested the crops belonging to the Burrs, which occupied about five days, and then returned to Randolph. Mr. Harris remained about five weeks, his dog being his sole companion during the whole time, except the five days that Burr and Sears were with him; his only bed

HARRISVILLE.

being an old wagon board, each end of which was so supported that it had a sort of spring motion, which Mr. Harris says he is quite certain had as sure an influence to induce quiet repose to him at that time, as would one of "Howe's improved Eliptics" to the most elite and fastidious of modern dandies.

On the return of Mr. Harris to Portage county, he first learned of the surrender, by Hull, of Detroit, to the British, and at a call from General Wadsworth the militia on the Reserve turned out *en mass*, and **Harris** with Burr and others were out in the campaign some three weeks, in and about the vicinity of Cleveland. About this time the Corbins sold out, and Russell Burr returned to Connecticut, leaving only Harris and Geo. Burr with their families, of all that remained of the infant settlement. Arrangements being made for returning to Harrisville, they left Randolph about the first of October, 1812, and again arrived at their homes in the wilderness in safety, finding everything quiet and unmolested. Being almost entirely isolated from the busy world around them, and away from post roads and post offices, they could of course know little or nothing of what was transpiring outside of the settlement, and necessarily lived in that uneasy state of uncertainty, which to be fully realized must be experienced. Yet nothing occurred to disturb their quiet until sometime in the latter part of November, when in the early part of the evening was heard what was supposed to be the shrill whoop of an Indian easily discerned to be in an easterly direction, and supposed to be about a half mile distant. Mr. Burr, whose house was the nearest the point from which the whoop seemed to come, hastily siezed his rifle, and taking his wife and child instantly started for the Harris' giving Harris' old horse, which was quietly feeding in the woods, a sufficient fright to send him on a keen run towards Harris' house, rattling his bell as though Old Nick himself was at his heels, thoroughly rousing the Harrises together with the old dog, who barking and bouncing through an old slashing, met Mr. Burr and added to his excitement by not appearing in his own colors, having been transformed into a snowy whiteness by some flour Mr. Harris had been shaking from his meal bags in order to fill them with grain, to be taken the next day to Middlebury. In the mean time Harris had not been a disinterested spectator. At almost the same instant the whoop was heard, and before its echoes had died away in the distance, he had seized his gun examined its condition, extinguished the light in his cabin, and sallying out in the dark proceeded at once up the trail in the direction of the Burrs, whom he soon met, when all returned to Harris' house, where the women remained while the men posted themselves at the corners of the house, to await further developments. In the mean time the whooping had ceased and everything remained quiet and still as though the angel of death had really reigned over the scene. Presently footsteps were heard in the distance; they approach nearer; the little band are all eyes and ears, expecting every moment to see spring out of the dark forest the still darker foe. Soon the dreaded apparition of some one in human form was dimly seen through the darkness, approaching the house, and when it was in hailing distance, Harris drew up his rifle and hailed. The response was, "Why, God bless you, don't you know Billy Thornington!" while all admitted that a better denouement could hardly have been given to the event.

On the first day of January, 1812, the deep snow of that year commenced and fell to the depth of eighteen inches. Severe cold weather set in and continued without loss of snow, until the 27th of February. On the night of the 6th of that month, a man arrived at the house of Mr. Harris and informed him that Mr. Henry Chittenden, in charge of five teams loaded with forty barrels of flour, being forwarded by Norton and Adams, contractors at Middlebury, to General Perkins' camp, on the Huron River, were detained by the deep snow, in the wilderness in the neighborhood of the Chippewa, and were entirely destitute of forage and provisions, having been five days out from Middlebury, and urgently soliciting Mr. Harris to proceed at once to the camp and relieve them. Food for the men was immediately provided by the ready and willing hands of Mrs. Harris. Then saddling his horses and taking on a bag of corn for the teams, with the food so kindly provided for the men, Mr. Harris, accompanied by the messenger, started about midnight for the camp, where they arrived at about four o'clock in the morning.

The reader can better imagine than pen can describe their reception at the camp. Suffice it to say, the courtly rules laid down by Lord Chesterfield were utterly discarded, while gratitude and thankfulness were heartily manifested in a manner more compatible to pioneer life. They were now only thirty-two miles from Middlebury, and had yet to travel forty-five miles through an unbroken wilderness, to reach the camp of the American army on the Huron river, with over-loaded and under-fed teams. Their only reliance seemed to center on Mr. Harris, his being the only settlement on the route. Mr. Hrrris, therefore, furnishing provisions for the men and forage for the teams, and lessening their loads by taking a portion with his own, started the next day for the camp at Huron, which they reached at the end of eight days, having camped out eleven nights in going and returning. Mr. Harris made the return trip in four days. The teams from Middlebury and Cuyahoga Falls continued the transportation of stores to Perkins' camp until about the 20th of February, making their trip much more expeditiously after a road had been cut through and a path well beaten. The time of the drafting militia at Huron having expired about the first of March, those from the counties of Wayne and Knox, together with other south-eastern counties, were obliged to pass through the settlement at Harrisville, in returning to their homes. Mr. Harris often entertained companies of from ten to twenty at a time, and furnished them the best his scanty board afforded.

About the first of April, 1813, Jesse and Theophilus Cross came from Randolph to Harrisville to make inquiries, and search for their father, who, with his son Samuel, left Randolph sometime in the preceding December, with two loads of oats, drawn by six yoke of oxen, to dispose of them to the Pennsylvania volunteers. They learned at Canton that their father had disposed of his oats on condition that he would deliver them at Mansfield; and as he did not return, his friends at Randolph supposed he had gone on with the troops to Fort Meigs. Subsequently learning he had not gone in that direction, they on inquiry found out by Mr. Crawford, the landlord at Wooster, that they had staid with him over night on the 31st of December, and on New Year's morning started for Harrisville with seventeen head of cattle, which he purposed to feed during the winter on the corn he had purchased of the Corbins.

On the next morning after the arrival of the Crosses, they, in company with Mr. Harris and Geo. Burr, proceeded to search for the missing man—having strong suspicions that they must have been in the neighborhood, from the fact that sometime during the month of the preceding January, some three or four head of stray cattle had come into the settlement. While prosecuting the search, and coming to the little Killbuck near the present site of James H. Moore's factory, they found where two yoke of cattle had been chained to saplins. At one place was found a yoke and chain, at the other the chain only; the cattle having probably managed to free themselves. Continuing the search in a south-easterly direction, to the vicinity of where Levi Chapman now lives, they found one yoke of oxen dead in the yoke. Appearances indicated that one of the oxen must have survived his mate sometime, having evidently drawn him about by the yoke a great distance. Here were also found the dead bodies of five or six head of cattle. At a little further beyond this point, appearances indicated that some one had evidently attempted to kindle a fire, small dry sticks having been collected for that purpose. Here was also found an overcoat, recognized as belonging to the unfortunate Cross, with fragments of other clothing, also a skull bone. The remains were brought into the settlement and buried. The supposition in relation to this sad calamity, was, that coming up from Wooster through the wilderness, he got benighted in the neighborhood of the Little Killbuck; that he there chained up a part of his cattle and undertook to come into the settlement, but being unacquainted with the location, and a severe snow storm prevailing at the time, he lost his way, and perished from cold and exposure, together with his son, and were mangled and devoured by beasts of prey.

In February, 1814, Russell and Justus Burr removed with their families, from Litchfield county, Connect-

HARRISVILLE.

icut, and located themselves in the immediate vicinity of Mr. Harris; and in the month of March, James S. Redfield returned to Harrisville, being then about fourteen years of age, making his home in the family of Mr. Harris. In April, 1814, Timothy Munson, from Vermont, and Loammi Holcomb, from the State of New York, with their families, settled in the west part of the township on the Black River. The township now began to receive a considerable number of permanent settlers. Among those who arrived in 1815, were Timothy Burr, Alvia Loomis, Collins Young, and Job Davis, with their families; and in 1816, Carolus Tuttle, Isaac Catlin, Nathan Marsh, Elisha Bishop, Perez and Nathaniel Rogers, and James Rogers, who drove the first loaded team over the site of Medina County seat, and whose wife was the first white woman that saw the site that was located for the old Court House. During this year also, Charles Lewis, David Birge, Josiah Perkins, and William Welch, moved their families into the settlement. In 1817, Noah Kellogg, Jason Spencer, Noah Holcomb, Thomas Russell, Isaac Rogers, Orange Stodart, Daniel Delvin, Henry K. Josline, Cyrus and Arvis Chapman, Jonathan Fitts, David Rogers, Cyrus Curtis, Geo. Hanna, and Doctor Wm. Barns, who built the first mill in the township, combining in himself the three professions of miller, doctor and preacher. The township was organized in 1817, being composed of the territory now included in the townships of Harrisville, Westfield, Lafayette, Chatham, Spencer, Huntington, Rochester, Troy, Sullivan and Homer. Isaac Catlin was elected the first Justice of the Peace; Carolus Tuttle, the first Constable; Timothy Burr, the first Township Clerk, and Joseph Harris, Loammi Holcomb, and Isaac Catlin the first Trustees.

HARRISVILLE.

In the spring of 1817, a small log school house was erected on the farm of Timothy Burr, near the center of the township, and a school was taught during the summer by Miss Diadema Churchill, which was probably the first school taught in Medina county, and the gem of our present elevated and flourishing Common Schools. Miss Churchill was soon after united in marriage with Mr. David Birge, being the mother of four children by this marriage. Mr. Birge died in 1825. Subsequently Mrs. Birge married a Mr. Gardon Hilliard, of Wadsworth and moved to Canada. The first church was established on the 3d and 4th of October, 1817, by the Congregationalists, on the old union plan, in accordance with which plan it soon united with the Presbytery. It was formed by the aid of the Reverend Messrs. Luther Humphrey, of Burton, Geauga county, and Amasa Loomis, a missionary sent out by the home missionary society of Connecticut. The organization took place in the little log school house already mentioned, and consisted of twelve members, viz. Isaac Catlin, removed to Michigan and died in 1856.

Eunice Catlin, died in Harrisville in 1834.

Loammi Holcomb, died in Harrisville in 1834.

Hannah Holcomb, still lives united with the Baptist Church by letter.

Nathan Hall, first Deacon, removed to Michigan, now living.

Pemilri Hall, removed to Michigan, now living.

George Burr, now a deacon, still living in Harrisville.

Mehetable Burr, died in Harrisville in 1843.

Russel Burr, died in Harrisville in 1834.

Carolus Tuttle, still living in Harrisville.

Cyrus Curtis, removed to Pennsylvania, and died.

The first settled minister in the township was the Reverend Mr. Breck, a Presbyterian clergyman. Other ministers of the Baptist, Methodist, Episcopalian and Universalist orders often held meetings in the township, as early as 1816. In 1818, Somer Griffin, with his wife, six sons and one daughter, moved into the township, also Reuben Chapman with his sons Levi, Perrine and Leonard, Captain Ed. Harris and family, David Sausman, Mordica Tracy, Stephen Harrington, with his sons Reuben, Benjamine and Weava Harrington. The first death in the township occurred in the person of a child of George Burr in 1817. Doctor Barnes preached the funeral sermon, being the first funeral service performed in the township. The first adult that died in the township was Hulda the wife of Stephen Harrington. She died in 1818. The first birth in the township was a daughter to George and Mehetable Burr, in the spring of 1815. The first male born in the township was Alpha, son of Justus Burr, now of Illinois.

The first wedding in the township was celebrated in November 1816. The parties to it was Levi Holcomb and Laura Marsh. There being no clergyman or Justice of the Peace in the township to solemnize the marriage contract, Mr. James Rogers, who still lives in the township distinguished now as then for his disinterested philanthropy in matters of that kind generously volunteered his services to procure the so much needed official dignitary. Setting out on foot, like Japhet in search of his father, he bent his course towards Wadsworth. Arriving there he made application to Esq. Warner, who readily assented to come out the next day and legalize the ceremony. It being near sundown Mr. Rogers, at the request of Mr. Warner, consented to tarry over night and accompany him to Harrisville the next day. But alas! how precarious are all human calculations. for during the night Esq.

Warner was taken so severely ill, that it was quite impossible for him to fulfil his engagement. Here was a dilemma. The wedding was set for that very night, and no one yet secured to perform the ceremony: but Mr. Rogers, whose perseverance was only equalled by his philanthropy, true to his purpose as the needle to the pole, pushed on to Esq. Van Heinans in Norton township. The Esquire, who as it would seem, must have been a lineal descendant of Nimrod, was out on a deer hunt, and did not return until night, when he very ungallantly informed Mr. Rogers that he was not at his service. This to most men would have been a settler. Not so to Rogers, these reverses and backsets only stimulated his zeal the more, for on learning that there was a Justice of the Peace in Coventry, he immediately proceeded thither, secured the services of an Esquire Heathman, and arrived at Harrisville the next day after the wedding — should have been. — However the affair was closed up that evening, and the parties are now living in Michigan. This is supposed to have been the first wedding in the county.

The first frame building in the township was a thirty by forty foot barn, erected by Russel Burr, in 1816, and soon after, in the same year, L. Holcomb built another in the west part of the township.

James S. Redfield brought into the township, in 1820, the first stock of dry goods and groceries. In 1826, Redfield and Chapman sold goods in company. In 1828, a store was opened by Barker and Siza, and in 1830, another by Archibald Miles and Charles R. Deming. Since that time, J. Higbee and the Ainsworths have been the principal merchants at the center of the town.

In settling a wilderness county, even those who have not experienced its trials and privations can easily perceive that the life of a pioneer cannot be one of entire idleness and inactivity. Roads have to be opened, farms cleared up, buildings erected; all this requires energy and perseverance. So it was in Harrisville. Roads had to be opened leading to Medina, Wooster, North to Elyria, East to Middlebury. Some were done by legislative appropriations, and some by voluntary donations. The road leading to Medina was a state road, for the opening of which the Legislature made an appropriation. James S. Redfield, in the spring of 1816, took the job of chopping out the road from the center of the town to the south west corner of Medina, and for making fifty-seven rods of bridges and causeways, and finished it about the first of September. Mr. Redfield says that the first loaded teams that passed over the road were those of Josiah Perkins and Titus Stanly, then moving into Harrisville.

The early settlers experienced much trouble in protecting their hogs and sheep from the ravages of bears and wolves, which infested the woods in great numbers, and many are the anecdotes related in relation to their encounters with them. James S. Redfield caught, in a period of a very few years, one hundred and twenty-two wolves, on which he received a bounty of——dollars each. Wolves, as Davy Crocket would say, are naturally a sneaking cowardly *varmint*, seldom attacking persons unless compelled by hunger. Mr. Redfield relates that having caught one in a steel trap by the end of the toe, and fearing that in its struggles it would get its foot out of the trap, he pounced upon it, put the foot of the wolf into the trap and carried it into the settlement. This wolf it would seem, was almost as passive as was old Put's, when he applied the torch to its nose, for it offered no resistance, nor manifested any viciousness except growling and snarling whenever Redfield set him down and attempted to make him walk, which Redfield says he very soon made him shut up by cuffing his ears. Judge Harris relates that being in company with Loammi Holcomb, about Christmas, in 1817 or '18, and in the vicinity of Campbell's Creek, in the township of Westfield, he there counted twenty-seven wolves in one drove. In 1818, a grand wolf hunt was projected by the townships of Westfield, Lafayette, Chatham, Spencer, Homer, Montville, Guilford and Harrisville, for the purpose of destroying and driving out those troublesome beasts, but as it is reported that no wolves were captured, the inference of the writer is that the benefit that accrued if any, must have been in the driving out process. However there is no doubt but that while no wolves were caught, many deers were, which with the excitement attending festivities of that character fully reimbursed the hunters for the fatigues of the day. Many of the early settlers are still living in Harrisville, among whom may be mentioned Judge Harris, George Burr, James S. Redfield, Timothy Burr, Albert Harris, who was a small child some two years of age, when his father settled in the township, also, Carolus Tuttle, James Rogers, Lomer Griffin, Levi Seva, Perrin and Leonard Chapman, Ebenezer Munson, Willis and Ralzmund Griffin. One notable fact of all others, and one which I am led to think has not a parallel in the history of many townships, is that of the four persons which constituted the first family in the township, all at the end of nearly half a century are now living in the township. They are Joseph Harris and wife, Albert Harris and James Redfield.

HARRISVILLE STATISTICS.

PERSONAL PROPERTY.	Number.	Value.
Horses,	545	$26,800
Cattle,	1,660	16,632
Sheep,	4,895	8,712
Hogs,	1,003	2,926
Carriages and Wagons,	176	2,789
Merchandise,		4,600
Moneys, Credits,		27,480
Butter, pounds,	59,710	5,970
Cheese, "	12,117	780
Wheat, bushels,	16,980	16,980
Corn, "	69,472	17,380
Total of yearly value,		$131,049

Making the average yearly yield to be $131,049 as listed and returned by the assessor in 1816.

If to the above be added the value that yearly results from clover and grass-seeds, oats, potatoes, garden and orchard products, the yearly amount of all would be about $175,500.

If the amount originated from the operation of mills, tannery, foundry, and other industrial establishments could be added to the above, the yearly amount would be largely increased.

HINCKLEY.

From the following narratives it appears that prior to 1818, very little was known of the township but what had been noticed and told by hunters, who when traveling had paid more attention to game, than to land, timber or natural advantages.

To those in search of level unbroken surface it did not seem very inviting. The many rugged jutting hills between which deep ravines intervene; and the long, high and narrow ridges of land made by the sudden circuitous windings of the Rocky River, from north to south, and then from south north-westerly, are calculated to give the hasty explorer unfavorable impressions.

But after industry and perseverance came and sheared off the forest, and permitted the sun to shine upon the earth's surface, it was discovered that the fertility of the soil was not inferior to that of lands south and west, and that the many springs of pure water that gushed from the hill sides at all seasons in the year gave strong proof of its being a healthy township.

Not a few, who preferred health to a level surface, made choice of the township of Hinckley as their residence, and the homes of their families for which they toiled. Since the first organization up to the present time (1861) the advances made in cultivation of soil, planting orchards, erecting residences and encouraging industrial establishments will make it compare favorably with other townships of the same age in the county.

The following narratives, compiled by Doctor O. Wilcox, Mr. Cogswell and Riley the Rover, comprise many historical facts worthy of being read. and preserved by the descendants of the first pioneers.

NARRATIVE BY O. WILCOX.

In the distribution of the lands of the Western Reserve, among the original land speculators who bought it of the State of Connecticut. the township of Hinckley fell to the lot of Judge Samuel Hinckley, of Northampton, Massachusetts. When or where he was born, I do not know, but he was educated for a lawyer and as I understand began life rather poor. He amassed considerable property and died about twenty years ago, in Northampton, esteemed and respected by his neighbors for his many virtues. He had a strong penchant for trading in lands and it almost seems that Heaven would be no Heaven to him unless he could trade in land there, as is illustrated by the following anecdote which is related of him.

Governor Strong, of Massachusetts, was a brother-in-law of Hinckley, and also owner of lands on the Reserve. One day they were discussing the propriety of putting their lands into market. Strong thought it best, as the saving in taxes and interest would more than equal the rise in value. Hinckley dissented. "Why," said he "the time will come when those lands will sell for ten dollars per acre." "Yes," replied Strong, " but before that time comes, you and I will be in Heaven." "Ah! that's the Devil of it," said the Judge.

The Judge was owner of several townships and parts of townships besides Hinckley, and as this was a rough, broken township, he seemed to think less of it than he did of his others, consequently he had them surveyed and brought into market first. Hence all the adjoining townships were partially settled before Hinckley. The wild animals, disturbed by the crash of falling trees, the barking of dogs, the loud shouts of merry children (the children were noisy in those days,) and the crack of the settler's rifle, fled from the noise and confusion to the silent shades and deep recesses of Hinckley, where they were comparatively safe from disturbance. Of course Hinckley abounded in wild game and this led to the getting up of a grand hunt. The great Hinckley hunt was the first incident in its history worth relating and as this has been so often and ably described by others; I will not write it, but leave the description to Cogswell and Riley the Rover, who are more conversant with its incidents than I am.

The hunt took place in 1818. The next year the township was surveyed by Abraham Freeze, Esq., of Brunswick, for the Judge. He made one hundred lots of it, each containing one hundred and sixty acres.

Lot No. One was in the north-west corner of the township, the next lot east was No. Two, and so on back and forth to the south-west corner of the township which was lot One Hundred. On lot Sixty-nine, Freeze found a squatter named Walton, who was the first settler in the township, and the only one at the time of its survey in 1819. Where Walton came from or where he moved to I never could learn. He was an industrious man and had made considerable improvement on what is considered the best lot in the township. Freeze paid Walton for his improvements and bought the lot of Hinckley, and afterwards sold it, about 1835, to

Nathan Wilson, who on his death left it to his daughter Julia, who is now its owner.

The same or next year, Frederick Deming, of Brunswick. bought lot Fifty-two and a part of lot Forty-nine and built in the south-east corner of lot Forty-nine. Here he lived almost alone for a few years. A Mr. Stillman bought the remainder of lot Forty-nine, and built nearly opposite Deming's, where Joseph Gouch now lives. A Mr. Beaumont, who was an acquaintance or relative of Stillman's, came with him and bought on lot Thirteen, where N. L. Usher now lives, and made some improvements. Stillman soon died—what year I cannot ascertain. Deming selected a knoll a little west of his residence for his burial. Here the Ridge burying ground is now located. The death of Stillman so discouraged his family that they moved back to the State of New York, whence they came, accompanied by Beaumont. Settlers gradually came in, among whom were Dorman Buck, Jared Thayer, J. Fisk, I. Loomis, A. Freeze, Ingersol Porter, D. M. Conant, Chester Conant, Easton, Piper, Stow and others; so that they thought it best to have the township organized and named.

The first frame barn put up in town was for A. Freeze; it was a large barn thirty-five by forty-five feet on the ground, and for all the work, which was done by contract Freeze paid only seventy-five dollars! At present prices of labor it would cost nearly double. At the raising of this barn, which was in the spring or early summer of 1824, and which required the help of all the able-bodied men in the township, as well as many from Richfield, the question of organizing and naming the township was discussed. Freeze stated to the people that Judge Hinckley had promised him that if the citizens would name it Hinckley in his honor he

would deed them a lot of one hundred and sixty acres
for school purposes, or any use they choose to put it
to. They therefore voted to name it Hinckley. The
next year when the Judge made his annual visit to
collect his dues, Freeze reminded him of his promise.
The Judge hemmed and hawed, said he had been very
unfortunate the past year, had met with heavy losses,
had had much sickness in his family, and really did not
feel able to make so large a gift; but he would donate
two and one-half acres at the center for a public square,
and two burying grounds, each containing one and one-
fourth acres, which was the best he could do: these he
accordingly deeded to the township. The first township election was held at the log school house built on
A. Freeze's land, the site of the present school house
in District No. One, September 25, 1825. Thomas N.
Easton, Jared Thayer and D. M. Conant acted as
Judges of election and Reuben Ingersol and A. Freeze,
Clerks. They elected Jared Thayer Clerk; R. Ingersol,
T. N. Easton and Josiah Piper, Trustees; Joab Loomis
and Samuel Porter, Overseers of Poor; Curtis Bullard
and Richard Swift Fence Viewers; D. M. Conant and
Jonathan Fisk, Listers and Appraisers of property;
Fred. Deming, Treasurer; Thomas Stow and D. Bab-
cock, Con-tables; John C Lane, Chester Conant, Abra-
ham Freeze, David Babcock, Supervisors.

Of all the above named officers, Easton, Piper, Swift
and Babcock only live in Hinckley now. Stow and
Porter died in Hinckley. The rest moved away and
have died or are living elsewhere.

Curtis Bullard was the first Justice of the Peace
elected, and the first couple he married, and the first
couple married in the township; were a Mr. Carr and
Miss Harriet Wallace. Wallace lived on the farm now
owned by Andrew M'Creery. Among the guests pres-

ent were Mr. Piper and wife; Bullard and wife, H. Bangs, E. Bangs, and others, and they had a right jolly time. Among other amusing performances they sang "Scotland is burning, run boys run, Scotland is burning, fire, fire, fire, Pour on water, pour on water," &c. They were excellent singers and carried all the parts to perfection. The time and occasion and spirit in which it was sung rendered it ludicrous and laughable in the extreme.

Carr stayed with his wife but three or four days and then left her for parts unknown.

The first child born in Hinckley was a daughter to Mrs. F. Deming. I can't ascertain whether that child is living now or not, but the impression of the neighbors is that she died when young, in Hinckley. The first school taught was in the log school house already mentioned, by Miss Julia Curtis, of Richfield. The house was built by Freeze and neighbors in 1824. To her went the young of the neighborhood, but of all that went and all that sent to that school, not one now lives in Hinckley. Miss Curtis married Erastus Oviatt, of Richfield. After Oviatt's death, she married Dr. Hiram Wheeler.

The Congregational Church was organized in Hinckley, May 5, 1828, with the following members: James Porter and Mary his wife; Cornelius Northrop and Mary his wlfe; John Jones and Myra his wife; Mrs. B. Thayer, wife of Jacob Thayer; Mrs. Temperance Easton, wife of Thomas Easton; Harriet Carr, wife of John Carr; Curtis Bullard, and Sarah his wife; Zilpah Loomis, wife of Jacob Loomis; Mary Fisk, wife of Jonathan Fisk; Thomas W. Easton and Samantha Loomis. Rev. Simeon Woodruff and Israel Shaler conducted the exercises at the organization.

The first frame dwelling erected in town was by F.

HINCKLEY. 109

Deming. It was burned down a few years ago, while owned by widow Sawyer. The next erected was by A. Freeze, which is still standing. The dwellings of the first settlers were universally built of logs. Though not as commodious as the present dwellings, the dwellers therein enjoyed as much true happiness. This all the old settlers will testify to, and that they were healthier, the bills of mortality will show. Hinckley was as populous in 1840, as now. The following bill of mortality carefully kept by Deacons Waite and Close, will show the number of deaths since 1840. This may be relied on as nearly, if not quite correct. There died in 1840, 9; 1841, 6; 1842, 7; 1843, 11; 1844, 12; 1845, 15; 1846, 17; 1847, 16; 1848, 22 : 1849, 13, 1850, 10; 1851, 10; 1852, 15; 1853, 11; 1854, 31; 1855, 11, 1856, 13; 1857, 11; 1858, 13; 1859, 9; 1860, 16; 1861 to August 18, 12.

The oldest person who died was Mrs. Damon, mother of the late Caleb Damon. She died at the advanced age of one hundred and three years. The next oldest was Mr. Brown, father of Mrs. Salmon King; his age was eighty-nine years. Of the deaths, some were accidental and violent. T. N. Ferris was killed by the fall of a tree; Richard Swift, Jr., was killed by the accidental discharge of a rifle in his own hands; J. B. Dake was killed by the kick of a horse; Caleb Damon was shot by A. Shear, while hunting turkeys. Damon had secreted himself behind a log, and was imitating the call of a turkey. This called up Shear, who was hunting, and who saw Damon's head move just above the log. Mistaking it for the turkey, Shear took aim, and on going to find the turkey he found his friend and neighbor in the agonies of death. S. P. Woodruff was killed by lightning, and some children have been so badly burned as to cause their death: so that Hinckley on the whole may be called a healthy township. The deaths scarcely averaging one per cent. If time permitted I might record some anecdotes, hunting stories and fun, but the above must suffice. The history of Hinckley does not abound with stirring incidents of field and flood. Such as occurred to my mind I have hastily written as above. I believe them to be generally correct. If I have made mistakes it is through misinformation and treacherous memory. After a lapse of thirty or forty years it is very difficult to get at the exact truth of things. I have enquired of more than a dozen who were present at the great hunt as to the day of the month it took place on, and but one pretended to know. He said it occurred on the 24th of December, for he recollects the next day was Christmas. Should a second edition be called for I may perhaps enlarge and improve — till then this must suffice.

THE GREAT HINCKLEY HUNT—BY MR. COGSWELL.

Game being numerous in this section, in 1818, especially bears and wolves, which were a great annoyance to the settlers, a big hunt was resolved on, and appointed to come off on the 24th of December, by a proclamation to the following towns: Cleveland and Newburg, who were to form on the north line of Hinckley; Brecksville and Richfield, on the east line; Bath and Granger on the south line; and Medina and Brunswick on the west line, and thus complete the square. It was the intention to sweep the whole township of Hinckley, and orders were given to be on the ground about sunrise. Uncle Gates and myself started from his residence, on the Cuyahoga river; the day previous to the hunt, with the intention of taking a little look for game through the woods as we went, and in order to be on the ground the next morning. When we were near the north line of Bath we separated with the understanding that we would meet at another certain point. I had not gone far, when I discovered where a coon had come off of a large oak tree, and had turned back and went up the tree again. I knew if there was an Indian there he would contrive some way to get the game without the trouble of cutting the tree. I looked about to see how this could be accomplished. There was a large limb on the oak, about sixty feet from the ground, and not far from the tree was a small hickory, which if fell would lodge on the limb. I chopped the hickory, it lodged, and made as I supposed, a safe bridge by which I could reach Mr. coon. But I was mistaken, for when within ten or twelve feet of the limb, I discovered that there was a very little of the top of the hickory that was above the limb, and that it was sliding down further every move that I made. This was a perilous situation indeed, and I saw that something decisive must be done. I first thought of retreating, but I soon found that this would be as bad as proceeding, as every move I made brought the hickory further off the limb. I therefore resolved to reach the tree if possible, and with several desperate grabs, I did so. I now thought I would make things safe, and I took the few remaining twigs that still sustained the hickory and withed them around the limb of the oak. I soon discovered the retreat of my coon, and chopping in I pulled him out and threw him down to my dog. I descended safely, and by the time I had reached the ground my uncle Gates came up. I showed him what I had done, and he declared that he would not have undertaken it for all the land on the Cuyahoga river, from Old Portage to Cleveland. I did not undertake it for the value of the coon, but because I thought I would not be outdone by the Indians. We stayed over night at Mr. Rial Bray's, near the east line of Hinckley. The next morning we were on the line by sunrise. We waited some time before they were all to their places, and then the word "all ready" was passed from mouth to mouth. The word was forty seconds going round the twenty miles, the first telegraph known. Then came the sound of the horns, which was the signal for a start. The managers had made a circle, half a mile in diameter, in the center of the town by blazing trees, and when we came to that circle we were ordered to halt. It soon became evident the ring was too large as the game had a good chance to secrete themselves. The managers now came to me and said they wished I would select some good man, and go into the ring and shoot some of the large game, which would drive the rest toward the outside. I selected my uncle Gates, and we proceeded toward the center. I soon came in contact with plenty of wolves and bears, and had shot several when I saw near the center a monstrous bear, I think the largest I ever saw of that species. I wounded him twice so that he dropped each time, when he retreated toward the south line, and I followed in close pursuit. About this time the south line advanced about forty rods, which brought them within a short distance of myself and the bear. My dog seeing me after the bear broke away from the young man who had him in charge, and came running to my assistance, and met the bear just as he was crossing a little creek on the ice. I ran up to the bank, within twenty-five or thirty feet of the bear, and stood several feet above him. About this time the men in the south line commenced shooting at the bear, apparently regardless of me or my dog. There were probably one hundred guns fired within a very short space of time, and the bullets sounded to me very much like a hail storm. As soon as the old fellow got his head still enough so that I dare shoot, I laid him out. While they were firing so many guns, a great many persons hallooed to me to come out or I would be shot, but as it happened neither myself nor dog were hurt, and even the bear was not hit by their random shots, for when he was dressed there were but three ball holes found in his hide, and those I made. I now returned to the center alone, as my uncle Gates had got frightened out, and finished the bears and wolves, then commenced on the deer. I killed twenty-five or thirty so fast that I did not pretend to keep count. I stood by one tree and killed eight as fast as I could load and shoot. The last animal that I killed was a wounded wolf that had secreted herself in the top of a fallen tree. We were then ordered to go down where the big bear was, discharge our guns, and stack them, and proceed to draw in the game. It was found, when the men were all together, that there were four hundred and fifty-four, and it was estimated that there were about five hundred on the lines in the morning. The amount of game killed was, about three hundred deer, twenty-one bears, and seventeen wolves, that were killed in the ring, and it was estimated that about one hundred deer were killed while marching to the center. The night was spent merrily in singing songs, roasting meat, &c. In the morning we tried to hit on some plan to organize, and divide the game, but it seemed impossible to get any plan to work. About this time Major Henry Coyt came from Liverpool, and I went and asked him to assist us in bringing about an organization. He did so and succeeded in getting a com-

mittee appointed, consisting of himself, Capt. John
Bigelow, of Richfield, and myself. We proceeded to
divide the men into four divisions, as follows: first
divisien, Cleveland, Royalton and Newburg; second division, Brecksville and Richfield; third division, Bath
and Granger; fourth division, Medina, Brunswick and
Liverpool; and then we divided the game as well as we
could in proportion. This was probably the greatest
hunt that ever has been, or ever will be in the United
States; and strange to say, but one accident happened.
Captain Lothrop Seymour received a buck shot in his
shoulder and one in his leg. I frequently heard bullets whistle near me, and saw one bush cut off by a
ball not more than a rod from me. Many of the proceedings through the night, I have not written in detail,
as it will probably be graphically given by Riley the
Rover, and perhaps some others.

THE HINCKLEY HUNT—BY RILEY ROVER

I was in the town of Hinckley
   A week or two ago,
And heard some good old settlers tell
   The tale I write below.

The scene that in this tale appears,
   You will please remember,
Lies in the past full two score years
   From coming next December.

HINCKLEY.

In all the towns that lay around,
    Many settlers had crept in,
And broke the forest with the sound
    That settlements begin.

They were a set of stalwarth men
    And had their past-times bold;
Wild beasts were in the forest then,
    As in the plains of old.

The township was a favorite haunt
    For game of every kind,
Where hunters weekly took a jaunt.
    Their quiet lairs to find.

As taught to shun the settlers door,
    Beasts from his cabin fled
This town became yet more and more
    The haunt to which they fled.

At length a message went around,
    To test the settlers sent,
To see how many could be found,
    To join a royal hunt.

We'll form, said they, a line of men,
    Around the town at morn,
And march straight to the center then,
    With whistle, shout and horn.

The proposition pleased them well,
    And all agreed to go,
Who had a gun, a voice to yell,
    Or konkle shell to blow.

They blazed a line around the center,
    Made plain to every eye,
To show where only beasts might enter,
    And not a man pass by.

The day was set, the dawn drew near,
    To game—the dawn of doom,
From every side the men appear,
    In mists of morning gloom.

From left to right they sound the horn,
    Till all their place have found,
And on the breath of echoing morn,
    The notes go quickly round.

Then every man his skill employs,
    Some frightful sound to try;
But none must light the firy steam,
    Nor let a bullet fly.

Until the signal at the center,
    Shall bid the circle round,
Upon the work of death to enter,
    And slay the beasts then found.

In droves of scores, the panting deer
   Sweeping the circle round,
Before the hunters shot appear,
   A mark at every bound.

It is a wild and thrilling sight,
To see the baffled herd's affright,
To see the eye-balls of the deer,
Out-straining from his head appear;
To hear old bruin's sullen growl;
To hark the wolf's despairing howl;
To see the hunter in his place,
Snatch up his rifle to his face,
The flash and dust and fire let fly,
With rattling echo's quick reply;
To see game stricken in their bound,
Fall noisless, lifeless to the ground
Or if they 'scape, as many did,
To see how quickly they were hid,
Without a pause to bid adieu,
As from the carnage scenes they flew.

Now thrilling scenes and sights are seen,
   Upon new work men enter,
And all more jovial than before,
   Drag game into the center.

But day turns on its dusky side,
    As they their work have done,
They wait till morning to divide
    The booty they have won.

Foreseeing this, they gather first
    From off the gory field,
The wolves they've slain whose hairy scalps,
    A county booty yield.

All these they give to a trusty man,
    Who with a horse and sled,
To buy a giant whiskey can,
    Off through the forest sped.

In time, the man was on the ground
    With all his team could pull,
Joyfully the jovial fellows found,
    He'd brought a barrel full.

They set the barrel on one end,
    And knocked the other in,
They used for tapster to attend,
    A ladle made of tin.

Then, whiskey made by honest men,
    Was drank by men upright,
And none would deem it hurtful then
    To drink on such a night.

Then every man drank what he chose,
   And all were men of spunk,
But not a fighting wrangle rose,
   And not a man got drunk.

They kindled fires o'er all the ground,
   And made the forest light,
The joke, the jest, the song went round,
   Through all that jovial night.

They skinned a bear and dressed him whole,
   But little did they eat,
More fond of fun and flow of soul,
   Than of the greasy meat.

The bear was fat as fat could be,
   Wrap't round him like a place,
'Twould charm an Esquimaux to see
   His robe of dripping grease.

One hunter with an oily chunk,
   Soon chanced to grease another,
Who quick resolved with pleasant spunk
   To turn and grease his brother.

Quickly others joined the fun,
   Saying that oil was good for hair,
Oil on the heads of all must run,
   And none his brother spare.

It was a night of great anointing,
　　A night of wondrous things,
Night of instinct appointing,
　　Great jubilee of kings.

Old bruin's fat was used for oil,
　　And whiskey used for wine,
Triumphant mid their slaughtered spoil,
　　They made their faces shine.

Most of that noble jovial band,
　　Have past from earth away,
Yet still some scattered o'er the land.
　　Are living to this day.

I have myself a hunter been,
　　And aided by my hounds,
More than one hundred wolves have slain,
　　On western hunting grounds.

And I have been a Pioneer,
　　From my young manhood's birth;
With owls and wolves all howling near,
　　While sleeping on the earth.

Still I am not a settler old,
　　Nor yet Old Settler's boy,
I am a rover wild and bold,
　　And roving's my employ.

If to the foregoing amount was added the sum that yearly accrues from the production of clover-seed, grass-seed, oats, potatoes, orchards and gardens, the products might safely be set down at one hundred and fifty-two thousand dollars.

Let those who resided in the township in 1819, when there were listed for taxation nine horses and fifty-two cattle, contrast *then* and *now* and they must acknowledge that the advances have been onward.

HINCKLEY STATISTICS.

PERSONAL PROPERTY.	Number.	Value.
Horses,	498	$26,075
Cattle,	1,735	22,167
Sheep,	6,394	9,479
Hogs,	338	1,252
Carriages and Wagons,	173	5,830
Watches,	41	486
Pianos,	6	230
Merchandise,		3,725
Moneys, Credits,		28,962
Butter, pounds,	73,250	7,325
Cheese, "	38,950	2,337
Wheat, bushels,	4,672	4,672
Corn, "	19,145	4,786
Total of yearly value,		$117,326

HOMER.

Many of the incidents narrated relative to the first settlements in Harrisville, embrace a portion of territory and some of the characters that are now in Homer township. For many years prior to township organizations the interests of the two were partially indentified.

The first opening within the present limits of the township, was made by Mr. Parks, who is still a resident. In 1831, the whole township was unsettled, with only here and there a few rude structures that had been erected by the migrating hunters for a temporary occupancy.

The original papers relative to the first township organization are lost, and the early history is given by a few old settlers from recollection.

The first child born in the township was Harriet Parks. The first school was kept by Mr. James Parks, numbering fourteen scholars, very few of whom are now residents of the township. It was not then considered too far to send children of ten years old, two miles, by a circuitous path, to the school, without shoes, and not unfrequently without bonnets.

The first township Trustees were Messrs. Tanner, Park and Wing. Asa Beard was the first Justice of the Peace. The first marriage was Charles Atkins to Elizabeth Campbell. The first acre of wheat reared and harvested within the township was cut by Mr.

HOMER.

Duncan Williams, who is now the owner of large farm within the township. The settlements were rapid and the openings and improvements now seen, give evidence of untiring industry; and should the same perseverance be exercised for the next twenty years, Homer township will vie with any of the older settled townships, in agricultural products. There is also a marked advance seen in the erection of dwellings and other buildings, in the planting and cultivation of orchards and ornamental shrubbery, and in the selection of live stock. Not unfrequently the cattle from Homer, exhibited at our Fair, have taken the premium.

In future time the commercial advantages that the agriculturtsts of Homer will realize, must consequently add to their wealth. Proximity to railroad conveyances south and west, afford encouragement to the farmers of Homer and Spencer townships, that their surplus trade can readily and speedily be freighted to market whenever the price will justify. The soil, the locality, and the industrial habits of those who own the land in the township, indicate that before many years Homer township will compare, in proportion to age, with any other portion of Medina county in agriculture.

Many of the farmers are of German descent, and are of that class who strive to make their fields a little more productive, by manuring the ground they cultivate. The soil is well adapted to the growth of wheat, corn and grass; and the rapid increase of cattle, hogs and sheep, give evidence that the owners of the lands know what kind of stock is best calculated to enrich the owners.

When the township was first organized there were only nineteen voters. When the lister traveled over the township to get a list of the personal property for taxation he returned seven horses and forty-two cattle.

Let the present owners of lands, now in the township, read the following statistical table, returned by the assessor in 1861, and compare it with the above return and learn the commendable advances they have made.

It is due to the citizens of Homer to say that there are fewer mortgages upon the real estate in that township that upon many of the older settled townships in the county.

HOMER STATISTICS.

PERSONAL PROPERTY.	Number.	Value.
Horses,	529	$27,787
Cattle,	1,469	13,513
Sheep,	2,685	4,155
Hogs,	1,049	2,396
Carriages and Wagons.	185	5,247
Merchandise.		1,230
Moneys and Credits,		25,174
Butter, pounds,	58,760	5,876
Cheese, "	36,960	2,450
Wheat, bushels,	13,447	13,400
Corn, "	62,251	15,560
Yearly product as listed in 1681,		$116,788

If to the foregoing be added the value that results from the cultivation of clover and grass seeds, oats, potatoes, orchards and gardens, they would yearly amount to $35,000—making the yearly value of the products of the township to be about one hundred and fifty thousand dollars.

LIVERPOOL.

NARRATIVE BY MOSES DEMMING.

At the age of seventy, being the third time a widower, I sit down lonesome and disconsolate to write a short history of my life. When I take a retrospective view of the many dangers that have beset my path, I am constrained to exclaim—Lord! how often hast thou been my Protector and guide!!

I was born in Southbury, New Hampshire county, Connecticut, December 4, 1777. My father's name was John. He was born in East Hampton, New York, in 1727, of Scotch descent. My mother's maiden name was Anna Knowles. They were the owners of one acre of land, and as mall dwelling where they raised and supported a family of four sons and five daughters. My father was in the French war, and during the Revolutionary war, was frequently called out on alarms. When Danbury was destroyed by fire, he was present under command of a Militia Captain, whose courage was not of that kind that gained him renown as an officer, being more inclined to protect himself behind a wall, than to show himself in open fight.

My father enlisted when over forty years old, being fired with that true patriotism that spurred on the men in those days to fight for family and for home.

Mother was feeble, but not disheartened. She toiled daily to gain a scanty subsistence for her large family. Father sent money frequently, to aid in procuring family necessaries. But the depreciated currency then paid out to soldiers (continental paper) was of little value, and it often happened that the month's pay would hardly purchase provision sufficient for one week. I have heard my mother say that once she offered the whole wages that father had received for one month for a loaf of bread, and could not get it. I can remember when turnips were our bread and meat, and if a thin slice of bread was obtained, it was considered a luxury. It was not unusual to go to bed supperless.

At the close of the war we were greeted with the return of our father from whose lips I have often heard details of the many and severe privations endured during the Revolutionary struggle. Father sold his pay that he received as a soldier, for two shillings and sixpence on the pound, and got in silver sixty dollars. This was considered a large sum of money in our family. Both my parents died in the year 1809, aged eighty-two and seventy-seven years. At the age of fifteen, I had been bound out to learn the Blacksmith trade. At the age of twenty-one I went to Waterbury. While at work there I became acquainted and captivated with Ruth Warner. There was something so pleasing in her manners and conversation that I could never forget her. After leaving that place I roamed from place to place, seeing new objects, and seeking new sources of wealth or comfort, and again returned home, not five dollars better off than when I left. It is true that while traveling I had sometimes a little good luck, again much ill luck. Sometimes enjoying pleasant seasons, then again it seemed as though the very elements opposed my progress. Deep snow, high waters, severe colds and mud were encountered by me in many rambles, and caused me to exert my ingenuity and physical power to advance. I now came to the conclusion that if I ever intended to prosper, I must cease rambling and settle down. I accordingly commenced my trade, used economy, and in due course of time could say that I was out of debt, and had some cash on hand. Thinking seriously that a stationary life and a suitable companion would add to my comfort I visited Ruth Warner, proposed, and was married to her June 1, 1802. I became the owner of twenty acres, which I improved and by diligence and the very prudent economy of my wife, we gained a good share of the necessaries of life. By industry we added twenty acres more to our original purchase. After some time I concluded to sell and seek land elsewhere. I found a live Yankee who offered to purchase and pay in wooden clocks. At first I declined to trade, having never seen the inner workings of a wooden time piece. In order to make myself acquainted with clockology, as manufactured under the wooden creed, I assumed the responsibility of taking my own apart, and examining its mysteries. I spent the main portion of the day in unfixing and refixing it, and then concluded that I was prepared, after serving an apprenticeship to myself, to repair wooden clocks.

Believing myself now an adept in the way of fixing clocks, I bought twelve clocks for one hundred and twenty dollars, and started out as a clock pedler. I remained abroad about six weeks and returned with cattle valued at one hundred and eighty dollars, having made about sixty dollars clear.

Shortly thereafter, I sold my 40 acres of stony, hilly, poor land for one hundred and two dollars, and agreed to give possession in one year thereafter, and started into Onondagua on a peddling excursion. I had, while traveling, contracted for and owned a small farm and dwelling on the east bank of Scanecttles Lake, about four miles from its outlet. Our new home was delightful and our neighbors truly kind and religious. To stock my new farm, I sold clocks for cattle, geese or any kind of trade that people would barter for wooden time-pieces. About this time my brother Davis and others had become deeply engaged in the making and selling Miner's Wheel-heads. As I had been successful in bartering clocks, I entered into the wheel-head trade and did a good business for some time. In course of time the wheel-head trade declined and eventually was placed in the same catalogue with wooden nutmegs.

About this time a religious revival commenced in our new neighborhood, and, thank God, myself and wife became converts. From then I date a new and happy era in my life. For many years prior I had been an open and bold infidel; looking upon professors as hypocrites and the Bible as falacious. From that period of my life, up to the present, I must say that the Bible has been my life chart, and the company of Christian people my delight, and after having lived on earth four score years I wish to bear testimony that in the religion of Christ there is a solace, a comfort that the world knows not. In the winter of 1810, Father Warner and Mr. Warden visited Ohio to look at Township No. 4, in Range 15, of the Connecticut Western Reserve, then in Portage county, (now Liverpool, in Medina Co.) Mr. Warner had corresponded with Mr. Coit, the proprietor, and learned the price per acre. In 1811, Mr. Warner, accompanied by Alpheus Warner and wife, and three young men as passengers, started for Liverpool. As they came by my residence, and had tarried with me, I was easily persuaded to accompany them. Father Warner and myself were supplied with clocks, which we sold or traded as we travelled. We arrived at Columbia on the last day of February, 1811. When at Cleveland, on our way to Columbia,

Mr. Huntington urged me to buy a lot in that town for $60, and pay part in a clock, and the balance in any kind of trade we then had with us. The lot offered to me contained one acre and a fourth, and is the same lot on which the Court House now stands. Cleveland was then reported to be sickly, and the scrub oaks seemed to indicate that the ground was too poor to raise white beans; so we could not make a trade. I traveled many miles over what is now called Columbia, Liverpool and Brunswick, exploring and deciding upon the most available portion to purchase and prepare to locate; and, after due deliberation, made choice of the farm on which I now (1860) reside. I contracted with a young man to make an opening and prepare a field to plant in corn the coming spring; and on 15th March started for home. Nothing of import happened on my way. When I got home I made preparations to move, selling off all that I could not take with me conveniently. I owned eleven head of young cattle that I determined to take with me if possible. Late in April we filled our wagon with such articles as we supposed essential, topping off our load with a quantity of wheel heads, and, hitching on a team of oxen and one horse, set out on our tedious journey. The driving of the cattle through woods and across streams, caused us trouble and toil. We progressed at the average speed of sixteen miles per day. Our wheel heads aided in paying our expenses at places where we tarried over night. From Cleveland to Columbia, a distance of twelve miles, there were no inhabitants, and in many places the roads were heavy. We traveled hard from early dawn to late eve in making that distance. The roads were very deep, and our chances to avoid deep mud, few and far between, unless we had cut an entirely new road. Prior to our arrival, there had been heavy rains, waters were high, and fordings rather dangerous. In attempting to cross a creek, the round poles composing the bridge were floating in an eddy over the two long stringers. I urged the cattle forward, and when they stepped on the poles they gave way and let the cattle into the water between the stringers. I stood on a stringer with a stout pole, pushed the head of each one of the cattle under the stringer and forced it through into the current, and by this means, after many punches with the pole and much grappling of horns, I got all my cattle over. We left our wagon, took a few of the necessary articles, traveled up the stream to where we found it more shallow, and after much toil and circuitous travel, we arrived at Liverpool on the 18th day of May, having traveled twenty days.

On the 1st day of June Sally Warner was born, and it may with certainty be recorded that she was the first child born in Liverpool township.

On 28th February, 1812, Father Warner came with his family and settled in Liverpool township. Our neighborhood was now composed of four families, and it seemed as though company was plenty. We were all friendly and all willing to aid each other. At this time I had in my employ a young fellow whom I had hired to aid in clearing land, and other services. His disposition was any other than kind. One day he seemed droopish, and I thought proper to inquire what was the matter. He showed me his hands and arms, when I made the discovery that he was literally splotched with itch, and his clothes were densely peopled with lice. To have him about my house in that condition would not answer, and I therefore set my wits to work to cure the disease and exterminate the vermin. Wife and self had some fears lest the red men might molest us, but when we found the itch and lice likely to be inmates of our cabin, we took courage, made battle by scrubbing and washing with ashes, sand and soap, any amount of hot water and bark ooze, and finally routed the enemies, who never returned to make a second attack. Our kindness to the fellow did not secure his friendship. Often, when driving the oxen, if he could find a hornet's nest or a swarm of yellow-jackets, it was his delight to drive the cattle among them and then witness the pain and misery he caused to be inflicted on the dumb animals. I sent him adrift; he got on board an armed ship, where he was guilty of mutiny, and was hung at Boston.

My wife who had been a sharer in the toils and incidents consequent to a life in the West, had declined gradually in health for some years. I had painfully watched the advances of disease, and although I used every prudent means to ward off the fatal shaft, I could not withstand the purpose of an over-ruling Providence. She died on the 26th July, 1812. Father Warner and myself selected the grave yard where we interred her. She was the first white person buried in Liverpool Township. Prior to her death, I had been busily employed in getting out timber for a barn, which was raised after her death, and was the first frame barn put up in the Township, and was the only frame barn between Cleveland and the River Raisin.

On the 4th June, 1812, war was declared, but our want of information by means of newspapers, prevented us, at first, from being much excited. We dreaded the Indians, but still supposed that those then at the head of our brave men would be able to protect us from danger. We had heard that Hull was doing good service and we reposed confidence in his valor. After the death of my wife I had hired Louisa Bronson to take charge of my house and to cook. One night when sleeping soundly we were all aroused by the rap of father Warner at the door, holding the unexpected news that Detroit had surrendered, and that the British were landing at Huron; that the people at Columbia were packing up to leave, and wishing us to be at T. Doan's next morn by sunrise, to go with them to Hudson. Miss Bronson commenced getting early breakfast. I commenced putting the hay rack on the wagon and fixing light puncheons as a bottom, (we had no boards) and by the time breakfast was ready we were ready to load the wagon. Then thinking our return uncertain, I turned all of my cattle into the oat-field and let my hogs roam where they pleased. We selected and loaded such household goods as we thought we should need. I had a traveling trunk in which I had kept all my valuable papers. I placed that trunk in the center of the floor so that I might not forget it when loading, but strange to tell such was our haste and confusion that we forgot that trunk and started, leaving it in the same spot where I had placed it. We traveled with one pair of oxen and a pair of young steers. In getting to Mr. Doan's, such was our hurry and confusion that we would travel through oat-fields or any other inclosure to shorten distance or avoid bad roads, and leave all fences down. By the time all had congregated at Mr. Doan's the number was considerable, including young and old.

We started on our retreat excursion in confused order, and our progress did not exceed two miles each hour. Mrs Scofield, one of our company, had an infant only three days old. In order that she might get along as comfortably as possible, her husband fastened a bed on a colt, got her comfortably seated on it, and he, leading the colt, kept up with the caravan. At night we placed no sentinels around our camp, for the reason that we had but one gun for all and only two loads of ammunition. About one o'clock at night Levi Bronson, returning from Cleveland, came across our camp and gave us the intelligence that it was prisoners that landed at Huron, not the British, and that we were in no imminent danger. This intelligence caused us to hold a council, and after various suggestions we came to the conclusion to return to Columbia and build a block house. The next day we returned and put in execution our resolve. The block-house was planned and erected, and Capt. Headley became the commander. One-half of the men were detained on duty while the other half were allowed to attend to their home duties. I made a practice of going to Liverpool every morning, when not detained on duty, and returning to Columbia in the evening. I drove my cows to Columbia, but fattened my hogs at Liverpool. They thrived well, though only fed once daily. All the women and children remained at Columbia for some time. Finding fear of the enemy subsiding, I came to the conclusion to stay and sleep in my cabin, with my dog as my only companion. In a few months I contracted with Mr. Morgan, to whom I rented my farm for four years, and being still a widower, and having no children to provide for, I concluded to seek some more settled and easy life. I went to Euclid and engaged to teach school. While there I came to the conclusion that I would cease to be a widower if I could find a woman upon whom I could bestow my affections. I became acquainted with Miss Clarissa Cranny, of Euclid, and we became husband and wife on 11th March, 1813. We returned to my farm the following April, bought back the lease I had made with Mr. Morgan, and re-commenced house-keeping. At the expiration of fifteen months we had a daughter born. For several days my wife was sick, but not thought dangerously so. But while hope seemed brightest, the night of sorrow was near. My second wife died and left to my care and keeping a helpless infant only a few days old. Her grave was the second in Liverpool Township. Mr. H. H. Coit had come and commenced digging for salt, and was a boarder at my house when my wife died.

My child was a great concern to me, and having tried several places where I had every evidence that she would be well cared for, I thought I would cease fretting, but when alone or when in company, I still felt as though I should make my home the abode of my child. I therefore came to the conclusion to seek a third wife. I had heard much of the character of Jerusha Russell, who was the teacher of a school at Newburg. She was a native of Windsor, in Connecticut, and had an unblemished reputation. I sought an interview and was successful. We were married on the 24th November, 1814. A third time I commenced adding to my improvements, and in all my efforts to gain necessary comforts, I was constantly aided by my wife. To me she was a faithful companion, and to my child she was a kind and exemplary step-mother. About this period in my western peregrinations and settlement, disease attacked my cattle, horses and hogs, which continued for two years. I lost within that period, seventy cattle, ten horses and all my hogs. The disease was supposed to originate from some poisonous weed or roots that decayed and settled in the marshy ponds of stagnant water that then were numerous along the river valley.

In the year 1816, the township of Liverpool was organized, with the following boundaries: Containing all the territory west of the Twelfth Range, to the fire lands, and all south of township No. Five, to the south line of No. One, being the south line of the Reserve, and being then a part of Portage county. H. H. Coit and myself were the two first Justices of the Peace, from which I derived no profit but much trouble. The territory over which we exercised judicial control was extensive, though as yet sparsely settled. When litigants came to me for law, I generally got the cases decided by a compromise, and closed judicial proceedings by feeding the disputants from a portion of my limited means, and sending them home friendly to each other.

I will here narrate the manner in which cases were decided when we did not wish our official duties to prevent us from attending to the more necessary duties of providing necessaries for ourselves. I had started early and traveled four miles to ask three men to come and help me roll some logs. When we got to my cabin I found a man waiting, whose face showed that he had been fully engaged in a fight. He said that he had come six miles to see me and learn what the law was as to Assault and Batterry, as he had been pretty well battered. The Bible was on a board which I wished him to take down, and read the law for himself. He took the book (I had no statute in the cabin at that time) and after turning over many pages, (I soon discovered that he could not read) he asked me on what page he could find the law of Battery. I told him I did not recollect the page, but I could give him the words of the law as recorded in that book. He said the law was what he wished to know, so that he might have some idea what sum he could recover from the man who had whipped him. I told him the words of the law in that book were; "He that smiteth thee on the one cheek, turn to him the other also." He looked at me, then at the book, took his hat and as he left said, that law was too devilish poor to do him any good.

I wish to close this hastily compiled narrative with a few personal remarks. My life has been one of change; I have tested privations; I have experienced afflictions; I have toiled hard; yet when I think of the privations, the afflictions and hardships that others endured, I must frankly say, that a kind Providence has, in my old days, blessed me with competence, and surrounded me with many friends. My prayer is, that those who follow after me may reap, from my exertions in former years, a full competence of the good things of life, and when they die, may they have the well grounded hope of a glorious immortality!

MRS. WARNER'S NARRATIVE—CHEESE MAKING.

Mrs. Warner, wife of William, had been reared in the school of industry, and when first settling in her wilderness cabin she plainly discovered that invention was as necessary as labor, in order that some things might be done. She thought her table poorly supplied if cheese was wanting. Knowing that her husband was daily employed, and had not time to attend to all that must be done, she undertook to make a cheese-press.

She rolled a short log to the corner of the cabin and fixed it firmly on one end, next she took a puncheon and placed one end in the opening between the logs and soon made the discovery that a few stones placed on the other end would create leverage. She used the rim of an old seive for a cheese-rim, into which she put the curd, surrounded by a cloth, placed that on the top of the upright log, placed the puncheon properly, put on stones at the extreme end, and soon had the satisfaction of knowing that cheese could be pressed and made. That rudely constructed press was used by her for many years, and she has the satisfaction of telling that from then to the present time (1860) she has never been without cheese, and that always made by herself.

To Mrs. Warner the privations incident to an early settlement did not seem insurmountable; and if any one will call now and see her, they will find her employed in making, planning, arranging and providing articles that are calculated to make any one comfortable. Things neccessary, useful and comfortable are such as she delights to have on hand.

When we came to Liverpool on 20th September, 1815, we began clearing off and erecting a hastily constructed cabin within a few rods of our present residence. During the day-time there were some rays of hope that prompted us to toil, but when the gloom of night surrounded our little cabin we often thought of the State from which we started, and the many kind friends from whom we seemed to be wholly separated.

After getting our cabin erected and completed so as to shelter us from rain and storm, there were many necessaries yet unprovided. For many months we were without a table. I had learned that a common white-wood table was for sale in Columbia, and I was determined to purchase it if within my means. Having brought my wheel and reel with me, I was willing to ply them for the purpose of aiding in the purchase of needed household materials. I got flax of Mr. Justus Warner and spun, with my own hands, twenty runs of linen yarn, with which I purchased the table. We't a d beds and bedding, but no bedsteads. Mr. Warner shaved walnut rails, nailed them together and made two bedsteads. When they were set in the two corners of our cabin and the beds made thereon we seemed quite comfortable, and things seemed to look neatly. The large chest in which we had packed and hauled our beds and fine clothing was placed on end in a corner and served us as a cupboard for two years. We had no coffee in our house for the first eight years. I had brought a pound of tea with me which lasted us over fourteen months. A rude grist mill had been constructed at Columbia where we got our scanty quantities of wheat ground. Once we failed to get our wheat ground, and were forced to find bread from some other source. I sifted the bran very carefully, of our former grists, (it was in the summer season and we did not then use bran,) from which I got flour that made us bread for several days. In the summer season I cooked, washed and ironed clothes out of doors without then thinking that the rays of the sun would tan my face and hands. Shoes I wore when visiting or going to church during warm weather, but when at home doing work about my house I could do very well without them.

When leaving New Haven county, Connecticut, I had packed up a small bundle of apple-seeds, and after we had about ten acres cleared I went out, in the season for planting tree seeds, and planted the seeds I had brought. The orchard now seen is the growth of those seeds. I name this to show what great accommodations in the future result from small means. Our grandchildren now eat the fruit that resulted from the care and labor of their grandmother forty-five years since. Mr. Warner concluded to build a barn and cover it with shingles. We had a fattened hog in the pen, which

LIVERPOOL.

he killed and hauled on a drag to Columbia and sold the pork, getting one hundred pounds of nails for three hundred pounds of pork, and felt satisfied with the trade. It took him a whole day to get to and from Columbia, because of the obstacles in the road. For the first set of tea-ware we bought in Ohio, I paid $5, which is still in the house, and at the present time would cost about $1 00. I have in my keeping a leghorn bonnet purchased fifty years since, that is worthy of examination by the ladies of modern times. The bonnet was once very fashionable, and for texture and shape was a model. I have also a wedding dress that forty-five years since was in fashion. I also have a tea-pot, sugar-bowl and stock glass that were in use more than one hundred years since. The modern belle when viewing such articles will learn what was commendable and attractive in the gala days of their grandmothers. In my early days I was a trained pupil in the school of industry, and taught that labor was commendable. Keeping that motto in mind I made it my duty to engage in employments that would be suitable and profitable. I now have counted my three score and ten years, yet in order to feel comfortable and to make life pass pleasantly, I work every day, not for gain, but for comfort. I still spin and make our wool into flannel, and would think it wrong to hire spinning while I can do it and be benefitted. I look upon labor as commendable, and while I shall continue to have health let me have useful employment.

The first sermon preached in Liverpool Township was at our cabin, by Rev. Simeon Woodrough. Although our house was small it contained the congregation comfortably. Mr. Warner spent a whole day walking and informing the neighbors that there would be preaching. At the first prayer meeting, the following was the order of exercises: Justus Warner read prayers from the Episcopal prayer book. Col. H. Coit read a sermon. David Hudson made some remarks and John Bigelow gave the concluding prayer. Episcopalians, Methodists, Congregationalists and Baptists all worshipped together at that first prayer meeting, and each one seemed ready to exclaim, "How good and pleasant is it for brethren to dwell together in unity." Could the same kind feeling influence now that then was manifest, contention, strife and jealousy would not rule to the extent it now does. It seemed to me that every petition offered on that day met the hearty amen of every person present.

In harvest seasons I have often assisted in gathering and securing our scanty crops. The cultivation in the garden was, for many years, left wholly on my care. Could the present generation see the wild state of garden and fields that once existed, they would be surprised. Stumps in gardens were many and not far between. In the fields logs and log-heaps were numerous. At night visits from the wild animals of the forest were frequent. Snakes were numerous and often came near, and even into our cabins. Our cattle often strayed into the wilderness, and caused much trouble to find them.

My race is very nearly terminated. I have lived to see the township densely inhabited, to see churches erected, to see roads permantly established, to see good school houses erected, to see farms improved, to see the wilderness disappear, and to see and know that most of the grand-children now living enjoy a competence that resulted from the toil and privations endured by their grand-fathers, and I, in my old days, wish them continual blessings.

HARDSCRABBLE—BY MRS. R. HINCKLEY.

Our duty is to follow our little band, as well as we are able, through early troubles, in a new settlement. Therefore we go back a half-century, to the State of Old Connecticut, in the town of Waterbury, at the house of Justus Warner, where we cooked the last Christmas supper, ere the departure of Justus and others for New Connecticut, as Ohio was by them termed. There the goose was dissected, the puddings done justice by, and after the Good-Byes, were passed as freely as the cake and cider which preceeded them, then came the packing and confusion incident to such occasions. Justus, with his son Alpheus, and Minerva, his young bride, equipped with two two-horse teams, with fifty long corded, wooden, Waterbury cloeks; two young men named Ely L. Seeley and David Scoville, took leave of their homes and friends with throbbing hearts and tearful faces.

To give our modern belles a minute description of the lonely young wife on her weary pilgrimage, would in all probability, disturb too much their nervous system; therefore we pass on, only noting one night's lodging, for example. We drew up at a small log tavern, (says our narrator) which was already full; but we brought in our own beds and distributed them about the floor, and ourselves into them to the best advantage. Justus being the olde', was entitled to the first chance in bed, and the courtesy generally accorded to women, gave her the next, or second place, and the husband was the rightful and lawful owner of a place beside his wife. The rest were bestowed promiscuously. And as the wood fire cast her fitful light athwart the wall, that young wife (after drawing up her feet, to keep them out of the ashes) "sought to lose in sleep awhile her useless terrors," and succeeded too; but ere long, a large sow with her family, forced open the door, and sought a place of rest also. In the act of rooting her bed, the sleepers were awakened. She being a large black animal, they supposed a bear was in their midst. So the cry of "a bear! a bear!" was sent up, and amid the uproar of the disturbed Irishmen, who came pouring down the ladder, and the hunting in vain for the gun, there was more diversion than sleep.

But morning came at last, and our party jogged on, changing wagons for sleighs, as the weather changed. Moses Demming had joined our party in York State, as he had married Ruth, the daughter of Justus, and was willing to try his fortune in the wilderness. An Irishman named Clark, was taken as a passenger, and thus, after fifty-two weary days' journey, we drove the cattle and hogs out of a miserable hut in Columbia, and pronounced ourselves the inhabitants thereof, until we could erect cabins of our own in Salt Spring Town, (for she did not yet claim the infamous cognomen of Hardscrabble.) The work of progression commenced on the place which we younger generations know as the Wetherbeck place. There a small spot was cleared, just large enough for our rude hut to stand upon, and when one-half of the roof was on, and as much of the floor was laid, we moved in. And then we fully realized "that poverty is truly the mother of invention."

We had rived out long shingles to cover our house, and they proved a great advantage to us in the formation of tables, book-cupboards, bed-steads, lounges, &c. Perhaps it would be idle to tell our fastidious ones, that our bed-stead had but one leg, and our table was made without castors, and the book-cupboard for the novels and stories of our friend Scoville, was a hollow log with shingle shelves. For chairs we used the boxes in which we had brought our clocks. Our implements for work, consisted of our axes and hoes we had brought with us, and a shovel belonging to Mr. Demming. There was an adz, too, which Minerva often used to good purpose on her rough floor.

So now our lady is fairly provided with her dower, with nature's wilds for her garden, the feathered tribes for her songsters, Indians, squaws and pappooses for her neighbors, let us imagine her doing the work for six persons, while we look after the male occupants of our mansion. Land was to be cleared; salt to be made; so in good earnest they went to work. Justus, with his teams, brought kettles from Canton, placed them on poles, and from the puddles of salt water manufactured salt. Wood was plenty, so it did not cost him much to keep his kettles hot, nor the housewife as many words as it does us of the present day to cook her fare. Our three young men, Seeley, Scoville and Clark, have begun chopping; and Alpheus, like the man we read of, had a wife, and could not work. But Mr. Demming had gone back to fetch Ruth to be company for Minerva, the lone woman of the wilderness; so I suppose she sang, or might have sung—
> "Hope, thou bird of the golden wing,
> Thou art ever hovering o'er us;
> Thou dost many a song of rapture sing,
> Telling of joys before us."

But at last she came, and in less than one month there was another visitant in the rude log cabin. A "wee thing" came, and the mother's heart was stirred, and the fountains of affection awoke. Sally Urania the baby was christened, and she was the first child born in Medina county, and her children's children sat upon their great, great grandfather's knee, and formed the fifth generation. Our family now consisted of nine persons.

The work of cultivation still went on. Minerva, with a case-knife made trenches and planted apple-seeds which her children of the fourth generation now in 1860 frequently eat of. Our garden spot was cleared and planted with all the various kinds of seeds which we had brought with us, sixty different kinds in all. Six acres was cleared and planted with corn. Justus passed most of the summer in trying to turn Rocky River in her course, but all to no purpose, for what with fever and ague, and very little calculation, he brought nothing to pass. Fall saw him on his journey back to old Connecticut after his family. Seeley, Scoville and Clark left also. Moses Demming had begun keeping house by himself, Oliver Terrill was hired by Alpheus to do a job of chopping, and at Christmas there was to be something done in the then wilderness, to hand down to posterity. So every man then in town, which was Oliver, Seeley, John Jacobs and Alpheus, all chopped at once on a large oak tree near where Hubbard's house now stands, and every woman, which was Ruth and Minerva, looked on to see it fall. The first cut made one hundred and sixty rails. The weather was so warm that baby needed a parasol over it to keep the sun off, and so cold in Connecticut that the illumination was given up—so said the letters of Aaron and Minerva. Then came supper, and the wild turkey was roasted, the wild jokes were cracked, and the wild laughter rang out through the wild forest, and every man, woman and child sat around the shingle table of our hostess. So much for Christmas.

Think not, dear reader, that starvation stared us in the face. No, no, the wild bees afforded sweets for our table, the seeds we had brought and planted had provided pumpkins for pies, the marshes yielded cranberries for our desert, our cow was cream for our tea, and we did not lack meat, for game was plenty, and we made our own salt to salt it with; add to these a good supply of wild plums, grapes, pawpaws, mandrakes, blackberries, raspberries, billberries, crab-apples, gooseberries; and wild hops for both beer and bread, a variety of nuts to lay by for winter use, and we have food worthy to be eaten on the large clean chip for a plate, with a sharp stick for a fork, and a pocket knife for a carver, as was often done when in the course of events the dishes brought with them had become broken. A hard shell of a squash served for a sugar-bowl, gourds were used for dippers, and many other things were substituted for things worn out.

Oliver and Seeley were one day chopping about a half a mile from the house, when Oliver, by a miss stroke, laid the edge of his ax into his foot, making a horrible wound. Seeley took him on his back and carried him home, only stopping once to rest on the way. Oliver weighed one hundred and ninety-two pounds at that time. Minerva and Seeley dressed the foot, and in time it got well.

Spring brought Justus and Urania his wife, with Aaron, Adna, Justus, jr., and Joanna, their children, back to Salt Spring Town.

Perhaps it would not be amiss to give our readers a few of the many little anecdotes concerning Justus, or Grandpa, as he was universally called. He had a very peculiar laugh, a very peculiar mode of expression, and was withal a very peculiar man. He was not a man given to profanity, yet in cases of great emergency he was known to vigorously ejaculate, "the devil!"

The old road from here to Columbia went along on the hog's back, west of **Mr.** Spooner's house. All may now see that beautiful hill, and they will also see one little rise, then a valley of some length, then another little hill. From the top of one of these hills to the top of the other Aaron and Adna had trained the old horse to go with railroad speed, always stopping at the end of his race course. So one day Grandpa set forth on a journey to Columbia ; but as he ascended the hill, lo! the old horse struck into a dead run, and he hung on for dear life, only saying "whoa! whoa! the devil!" but his speed abated not in the least until he ascended the next hill and stopped himself. Grandpa looked about and repeated "ah!" very deliberately, and proceeded on his journey. The horse did not find tongue and tell of this, but Oliver and Seeley did, for they were chopping by the way-side, and but for them the secret might have remained with Grandpa and the old horse to this day.

Our family was now becoming larger, but aristocracy had not moved in. To give our readers a little sketch of the wardrobe of a squatter and his family, would perhaps, not be uninteresting to our fantastic hooped ones, in particular, for they may be able to draw a slight comparison. Behold, then, the father decked in a doe skin shirt, a deer skin vest and buck skin pants, and children arrayed in robes of the same material, sewed with the same leather whang as their thread was termed, and we have a more substantial wardrobe even than had our first parents with their aprons of fig leaves. Shoes were made of untanned leather, cut in one piece and sewed on the instep.

We come now to the summer of 1812. And now if our work was fiction and romance, we could write of sighing zephyrs and singing birds, of gentle slopes and flowery dells, with flattering swains and fainting ladies ; for our heros and heroines, we would marry some and let others die, to suit the convenience of our story. But no, our romance is but plain reality ; hardships endured by our own fathers and mothers, to gain for us, their children, a home. So we sit and listen with the deepest interest to the stories which they narrate, for their trembling steps and silver locks tell us we may not long be permitted to pen these things from their own lips.

Death came, and Ruth was wrapped in her winding sheet and consigned to the cold grave. A place was to be selected for a burial ground, for the hand of death was even in the wilderness. Grandpa and Minerva went forth to seek a place for her tomb. They came to our beautiful hill, covered then as densly with its trees and bushes as it is now with its monuments and marbles, its willows and roses, and its grassy mounds which mark the resting places of the long since forgotten. There on the most beautiful of mornings, they cut through the roots of the trees with an ax, and with a hoe dug the rude grave and shed the bitter tears of affection, and slowly and sadly they consigned the body of their beloved Ruth to the grave.

This was but the beginning of sorrow among us. War and its horrors stared us in the face. The mother clasped closely to her breast her babe; the lips of the father trembled and grew pale, and the young men grasped firmly their fire-arms to defend the helpless. Then all waited in an agony of suspense until tidings came that Hull had surrendered up his army at Detroit, and the Indians and British were just upon us, and we must leave for older settlements.

It would not be probable that all would give an exact story concerning those troublous times. And after forty years have passed, shall we expect no disagreement in the different narration by different persons? All could not be alike affected. Aaron says, Alpheus, after working some time to get things ready for a start looked up in astonishment and asked what the matter was, and what they were trying to do.

Minerva found candles, hid her knives, forks and silver spoons in hollow logs, put away things the best she could to leave; unpenned the pigs; uncooped the chickens; turned out the cows with their calves; ar-aranged the bed on the sled for the invalid mother, and all took up their march for Captain Pritchard's, in Columbia. They arrived there just at sunrise and breakfasted on melons which were brought out, and then journeyed on to meet the Ridgeville and Columbia companies on the corners by old uncle Oliver Terrill's. There we agreed to go to Hudson, and proceeded eleven miles on our journey and camped for the night. We stopped the noise of the bells on our oxen, ate our rude meals, and dispatched two messengers, Dr. Potter and Lathrop Seymour, to Cleveland, for farther news. A person was met bringing news that it was not Brittish or Indians, but Hull's soldiers on parole, so our panic subsided a little. In the camp was Minerva with with her babe, fifteen months old; the wife of Scoville, with her infant, one week old, and another child two years old, and she and her two little ones sick with fever and ague, besides the rest that camped there. The horror of that night we cannot imagine, neither can pen describe it.

Morning saw us on our way back, but when we arrived at Jim Doan's, bad news again met us, with invitations from Cleveland and Euclid to come there for protection. As they were all together, a council was held, and some were for a block-house in Columbia, some for Euclid, some for Cleveland. Demming and Oliver went back to Salt Spring Town. Justus and Alpheus, with Scovill, and their wives, went to Hudson. The women staid seven weeks, and the men went back and forth, till Minerva came back, and order was a little nearer restored. But still there was a great fear of being slain or massacred by the Indians. Part of our men boiled salt while others slept; those that boiled always keeping watch for Indians.

Neighbors now began to move in, and peace and prosperity once more began to shine upon us. Adna and Robinson kept bachelor's hall in a shanty seven feet square, on the Wolf place, until Adna got tired of it and left Robinson alone. Grand-pa kept house on the Wetherby place, Alpheus and Minerva on the corners by aunt Sally's, Aaron and Lucinda on the place they now own, Demming and Clarissa (his second wife) on his present farm, down by the river. Wilmot, Noah and John Mallet moved in, and at this time Justus (or grandpa) began making improvements in his salt works by digging on this side of the river, as the old horse was often out of sight, and the salt kettle he had proved by an actual demonstration would not float. One day he, with his son Justus, started to go across, but Old Rocky was on one of her freaks. Grand-pa stepped into his boat, took his paddle and began rowing for the other shore; but, in spite of him, his little craft fast headed down stream. He did not know what to do. Justus shouted orders from the shore to no purpose. At last grand-pa repeated a very vehement "ah!" threw his paddle overboard, caught the rope at the end of the boat and pulled with a vengeance. Justus ran along the shore to a bend in the river, the boat came ashore, and he saved him from being drowned.

Salt was readily exchanged for other things necessary to us. "There are boards now on my barn," says Aaron Warner, "which cost me one bushel of salt per thousand; and the nails to put them on with, twenty cents per pound, and brought them from Cleveland on horseback, being three days on the journey." Salt sold at $20 a barrel, and the price of an ax was $5.

But I was going to tell of his success with his well on this side of the river. Minerva warned him not to fall in and drown in his own well, as Haman was hanged on his own gallows; but he took no heed to her warning. There had been a fall of snow in the night, and grandpa arose early in the morning and proceeded to his well. Minerva was about breakfast, and the rest were asleep. Grandpa being gone longer than usual, she became alarmed, and ran to the well. His steps were easily traced there, and on looking in, there he stood up to his arm-pits in water, shivering and bibbering with cold. Minerva ran back, roused the men, and bade them take the ladder, on which they had descended from the chamber, and run to the well and get grandpa out, while she made him some toddy, and got him dry clothes. And when he had got over his bath, Minerva said, "I told you so." "Ah!" said he, "I didn't fall into the well, I didn't. I slipped in, I did; and I didn't think of Haman, nor Mordecai, nor the gallows. But I thought how near I came drowning, I did; and I s'pose you never'll forget gettin' your say, you wont."

We shall now continue grand-pa's story, giving many of his sayings in his own language; for all that knew him knew his mode of expressing his opinion. Two men had one day made a bargain, and, as is frequently the case, both had repented, thinking themselves cheated. So grandpa went and talked after this fashion to them. Said he, "You both made a bargain, you did; and ye both want to shlink, ye do. But ye needn't nary one on ye shlink; I'll shlink for ye, and ye may look out how ye trade to shlink, ye may, and take your property and go home." After he was eighty years old, he climbed an apple tree to shake it, and fell and hurt him. Thereupon Mr. Muddiman, the Baptist minister, went and told him that such an old man ought not to be so presumptuous. "Ah!" said he, "I always fell when I was a young man, if the limb broke, and I always expect to fall when the limb breaks, I do." At the age of ninety-six, says Aunt Roxy Worden, he climbed an elm tree, and cut bean poles in my yard, and four years later we all assembled to celebrate his one hundredth birthday. He asked what we were all there for, and seemed very well pleased. They brought him pen and ink, and he wrote in a legible hand, on a blank leaf, in Minerva's Bible:

Justus Warner, Aged 100 years.

The following lines were penned by Rhoda Hinckley on the occasion, although she claims no honor in the poetic line; yet, for want of something better, she gives the lines below:

> A hundred years ago to-day,
> "A child is born," the people say
> As on his mother's lap he lay
>   In helplessness and purity.
>
> To-day the people come once more,
> To see the little babe of yore;
> His head with Time is silver'd o'er,
>   In his second infancy.

None that his infant brow,
Can look upon his pale cheek now
Furrowed so deep with Time's old plow;
    For all are in their graves.

But he forms plans to buy and sell,
And will full many a story tell;
And thinks 'twould be "about as well
    To live a little longer."

He's no more willing now to die,
Although he's lived a century;
My gentle friend, as you or I,
    He clings to life as strong.

Five generations came to see,
And stood around their grandpa's knee,
And heard his stories told in glee,
    Of days when he was young.

To-day they come from far and near
To celebrate his hundredth year:
And list again his voice to hear,
    And sigh *a hundred years ago.*

    Twenty days later, and all that remained of the vigorous old man was borne through the broad gate, up to the green hill top, and laid beside the wife of his youth and his old age. And the bell in the M. E. Church rang its first death knell to the tune of a hundred years ago, and the pens of the future left to tell of his deeds in life, while the long train of mourners will long remember "Grandpa."

"We are very fond of comparison" as our dear friend Nep says, so we will give her description of Liverpool in the past and present.

Our noble town was then a wild,
    With forests cover'd o'er,
Where but few settlers' children played
    Around the cabin door.

Few and scatter'd far apart,
    Was the settlers' little band;
For the red man still a footing kept
    Upon his native land.

Where now your many meadows stand,
    Your lines of fence enclose,
The curling smoke from wigwam hut
    And Indian camp arose.

Where now your rustling cornfields rise,
    Where waves your golden grain,
The nimble deer unchased by man
    Leaped o'er the grassy plain.

Where now your stately fruit-trees are,
    Where now your gardens lie;
Was then a trackless wilderness
    Where beasts were wont to hie,

> Your mansions then were not as now,
> Built up with brick and stone,
> But with those rude unvarnished logs
> They builded them alone.

And now let us blush to own that we, as citizens of our flourishing and prosperous town, suffer Minerva, the woman who has endured so much, to lack the miserable pittance so necessary to her comfort, and much more, to lack those kind words and deeds so necessary to the happiness of old age. In our abundance we have forgotten that the midnight lamp, the tear dimmed eye, and the aching heart are the inmates of the little white cottage by the way-side, surrounded by its green trees, its neat flowers, and its little garden, hoed and wed by her own industry. There is not a field in sight of her but bears the marks of her labor in times past, while she goes forth, day by day, and earns her bread. And should sickness come upon her, dare we hope that her forty years of privation and hardship would gain for her more than a home in our County-house. Alas! for the inconsistency of perverted human nature.

OTTER STORY.—BY ASA MARSH.

I was boiling salt at the salt works, and Mrs. Townsend came after me to go and shoot an otter, as she had discovered one in the water. So I went and shot it and brought it to the salt works, whereupon Townsend came in a rage and took it away. I went after him and brought it back. Then he came again and with his ax cut it in two and took one-half away, carcass and all. I let him go and turned to the law for redress, got a writ of Justus Warner, and proceeded to trial. Justus their hearing evidence, gave decision that each had their just share; Townsend half for finding, and me half for shooting. So we each skinned our part and dressed it, and Hiram C. Stevens came and bought both our parts and sewed them together. So you have the otter story as it is, not as it is told by different story sellers.

LIVERPOOL SALT WORKS.

1. Now it came to pass that during the reign of James. sirnamed Madison, the people residing in the land of steady habits, being at peace with all nations, kindreds and tribes, grew and multiplied.

2. They added field to field and farm to farm, and their cattle roamed on many hills and grazed in valleys.

3. And tidings spread among the people that the wilderness of the Western Reserve could be made as was the Garden of Eden, for beauty and for riches.

4. And not a few, prompted by love of gain, and being wedded to filthy lucre, journeyed into the wilderness of Ohio, and returned to the land of steady habits, and said in the hearing of the people, that the Western Reserve was a goodly land, and could be made to bring forth abundantly.

5. So not a few provided themselves with oxen and wagons; and when they had packed their clothing, cooking vessels, tools and other needful implements, set their faces westward, and started on a forty day's journey into the western wilderness.

6. And not a few whose trade and business had been the peddling of " wooden clocks" and " wheelheads," journeyed westward and settled along the valley of the river called Rocky, and built for themselves cabins in the valley.

7. In those days the Aborigines, called Redmen, were wont to hunt on the high grounds and along the valley of the river called Rocky.

8. Now when those who came from the land of steady habits, saw that the land was well to look upon, and that it could be made a goodly heritage for after generations, they became anxious to become owners and inheritors of pieces of the Reserve.

9. And by epistles, sent and received, they learned the price at which the land could be bought, and a few came, and then, by epistle, asked others of the same Connecticut tribe, to come and inherit with them.

10. Now a man called "Justus" had plowed with the owner of a part of the Reserve wilderness, and had by trade and agreement become the owner; but not liking the sight of the Redman, the hugging of bears, the howling of wolves and the hissing of snakes, he had returned to the land of steady habits.

11. And in those days a man called Seba, the son of Seba had squatted on land, the ownership whereof pertained not unto him, only on the principle of "Squatter Sovereignty."

12. And on the same land where Seba, the younger, had squatted, was a spring, from the waters whereof the Redman had been wont to make salt. But Seba knew not where the spring was, though he coveted in his heart to know.

13. So the Redman spake unto Seba, saying: Pay me five large pieces of silver coin, and I will show unto thee the spring that is saltish.

14. Now Seba had not the pieces of coin that the Redman asked, and he was sorely puzzled and perplexed; and pondered within himself what he should do.

15. And he went to the house of Jared, who was

his neighbor, and communed together with him, and they two covenanted to pay to the Redman the five pieces of silver coin, who then showed them the spring.

16. And they dipped the tips of their fingers in the water and tasted thereof, and lo! it was saltish; and they two rejoiced together, as one rejoiceth for a first-born.

17. Now Seba and Jared were ignorant of the land belonging to Justus, because they supposed the owner to live about two days' journey eastward from the spring, and they were sorely puzzled to know how they might get a title to the land; and the thing vexed them.

18. And Seba said, Let us go and take counsel of Nathan, of the country called Columbia, for he is a wise and cunning man, and versed in the law; and the counsel of Seba pleased Jared.

19. So they went together to the house of Nathan, and told him all that was in their hearts.

20. And Nathan hearkened diligently to all that was spoken by Seba and Jared, and said unto them, I will see to it. And they left him musing as they went.

21. And after they had departed, Nathan, having saltish gains in his mind, saddled his ass, and, by night, traveled north until he came to the town where Jonathan, the scribe, lived, who had done much land business for one Simon. And Nathan and Jonathan communed long together; and Nathan besought Jonathan to aid in securing to him some right in the salt spring.

22. Now Jonathan was as disposed to have an interest in saltish speculations as Nathan, Jared or Seba, and he felt strongly inclined to make self-interest the ruling motive in saltish matters.

23. As soon as Nathan had departed, Jonathan

saddled his beast, got thereon and traveled eastward to visit Simon and commune with him on speculations of the saltish kind.

24. Now Simon was inclined, from long practice, to catch hold of any speculation whereby pieces of silver might be made, and, after hearing Jonathan, he covenanted to meet him at the salt spring, near the river called Rocky.

25. Now it happened that while these things were being done by Seba, Nathan and Jonathan in the valley of the river called Rocky, that Justus who, in those days, tarried in the land of steady habits, heard, by an epistle sent, that a spring, saltish to the taste, had been found on the land he had covenanted to buy in the valley of the Rocky River, and to which he intended to return and posusess.

26. So he put his house in order, saddled his beast and started westward on his journey to the Ohio wilderness, musing on salt matters as he journeyed.

27. And in due season he came to the place from which he had aforetime departed, and set himself to work to make salt, and conceived that thereby he would have much gain.

28. And as he sat and mused in the door of his cabin, in the cool of the evening, he looked out and beheld two men coming, and as they approached he knew them to be Jonathan and Simon.

29. Now Jonathan and Simon were confounded when they learned that Justus was the actual owner of the spring, and saltish speculations died in them as they hearkned to the sayings and intentions of Justus.

30. So Simon compromised with Justus and covenanted to give him many acres of the Ohio wilderness for a share in the saltish springs, and they three made an agreement.

31. Now they digged and dug and dug and digged until the well went down one hundred and three score and two feet from the surface of the ground, and the opening was wide.

32. Now Seba had, aforetime, planted corn and done much work near to the well, and had supposed that he should have some of the saltish spoils, but they gave him nothing, and he became angry and his wrath was kindled.

33. And Seba called on the four winds to aid him in cursing the well and the salt made therefrom, and he wished that the salt might loose its savor, and it was so; that it might loose its measure, and it was so; and that it might loose its weight, and it was so.

34. So after the anathema uttered by Seba, all who bought salt by weight, bought much bitters; and all who bought by the measure, lacked in quantity; and all who bought much, saved but little; and all the buyers murmured.

35. And Seba often mused upon the saltish speculation after this manner: I scrabbled hard to get the pieces of silver; I scrabbled hard to get the well for my own benefit; I scrabbled hard to get others to aid me; they have had a hard scrabble to get the well from each other; it has been a hard scrabble to make the salt, and a hard scrabble to save it when made. And all the people call the place Hardscrabble unto this day.

36. In due course of time the zeal to own salt wells along the river called Rocky abated, the desire to buy salt lands failed, the using of salt from the well that Seba and the four winds anathematized ceased; the men who had been engaged in saltish speculations abandoned the practice; and all who bought it, unitedly called it a Hardscrabble.

LIVERPOOL STATISTICS.

PERSONAL PROPERTY.	Number.	Value.
Horses,	357	$10,637
Cattle,	1,393	13,720
Sheep,	1,683	2,409
Hogs,	506	1,326
Carriages and Wagons,	198	3,684
Merchandise,		4,784
Manufactures,		3,680
Moneys and Credits,		29,780
Butter, pounds,	28,150	6,780
Cheese, "	16,890	8,780
Wheat, bushels,	6,780	2,860
Corn, "	35,120	975
Yearly product as listed in 1681,		$99,245

If to the foregoing be added the yearly products of oats, potatoes, clover-seed, grass-seed, gardens and orchards, it is safe to say that the yearly wealth resulting from personal property and products, is not less than one hundred and fifty thousand dollars.

A great change since the Warners, Demmings, Wilmots and other first settlers made openings in Liverpool township.

LITCHFIELD.

It appears from early records that the portion of Medina county now called Litchfield was wholly owned by Judge Holmes, of Litchfield, Connecticut, who caused it to be surveyed into lots, and an opening, or improvement, of several acres, to be made on the southwest corner of the Center, planted an orchard and erected a cabin. Some time thereafter, the land reverted to the State of Connecticut, and, under the supervision of Mr. Beers, acting School Commissioner, it was thrown into market. During the time it was under the control of Judge Holmes, it was generally known by the name of Holmestown. When controlled, thereafter, by Mr. Beers, he called it, on his surveyed map, Litchfield, and by that name it was known at the date of its organization.

For many years prior to its settlement by the whites, tradition says it was a part of the choice hunting grounds of the Wyandott Indians; and that their wigwams were seen along Center Creek, in 1822. Prior to that year, the settlements at Liverpool on the north, and Harrisville on the south, had begun to spread and drive out the wild game that had been the wealth and food of the Redman, and caused him to desert his rude wigwam and seek after game elsewhere. Mr. Cyrus Cook, wife and child, were the first white persons who came and made the first opening in the north part of the township, on the line of the north and south center road. He came in February, 1830. In May following,

Jonathan Richards, wife and three children, (Charles. Abigal and Julia,) Thomas Wilcox and wife, George Wilcox and wife, with two daughters, (Lucretia and Abigal,) Eliphalet Howd and wife, Asahel Howd and family, (Henry, Elizabeth, Caroline,) Judah Howd and George Olcott, came from Connecticut and settled in the township. About the same time, Henry Howd, wife and three sons, (Albert, John and James,) came from Sheffield, Massachusetts, and settled. The Howds began their settlement on the west side of the center road, near the creek, and Richards located on the opposite side of the road, about one mile north from the Center. George Olcott settled on the south-west corner of the present Center, and George Wilcox on west side of road, about one mile south from Center. In the fall of 1830, D. W. C. Dickeson, Jacob Road and Z. Stafford came into the township and became settlers.

In May, 1831, Lewis Finley and Asa Strait, with their families, became settlers, and were soon followed by J. L. Hinman, D. Pickett, O. Nickerson, W. Cole and their families. Mr. Hinman built the first frame house in the township.

Miss Jane T. Strait, aged thirteen years, was the first person who died in the township, on the 13th June, 1831. At her funeral was the first public religious service ever observed by the settlers. On the following Sabbath, Asa Strait, by invitation, lectured to the people, and may be said to have delivered the first sermon ever heard by the then residents of Litchfield township. If the names of all then present were called, how few would answer! The moral and religious influence that prevailed in New England was cherished with respect; and as the children, one after another, left the homes of their parents and became parents in the wilds of the Western Reserve, they came together and worshipped as did their fathers. When the morn of the Sabbath came, they congregated, not at the sound of bell, but prompted by the impressions made in childhood; and thankfully acknowledged the superintending care of Providence.

On 30th June, 1831, the township of Litchfield was organized, by electing E. Howd, J. Vandventer, George Olcott, Trustees; Thomas Wilcox, Clerk; Asahel Howd, Treasurer; and Jonathan Richards, Justice of the Peace. At that election, nine votes were cast.

In the month of May, 1832, forty-one persons came into the township in one day. Of that number, Messrs. Crow, Halladay, Wheeler, Peltons and their families comprised a part. So great a number soon gave life and power to the sparse settlers, and encouraged perseverance.

The fourth July, 1832, was celebrated by the settlers of Litchfield meeting, selecting a site, cutting and hauling logs, and building a log meeting-house. To give sanction to such work on that day, the good wives, at the appointed time, came with baskets of cooked provisions, and, with their husbands, ate thaukfully and joyfully, when they reflected on the prospects before them. At the same place, and on the same day, they formed a Temperance and Moral Reform Society, which grew in influence and in numbers, and may really be considered one of the very necessary aids of moral reform. Nine names were obtained to the Temperance Pledge on that day; and shortly thereafter, a Temperance Society was duly organized, which continued to meet and act until 1844, when its members adopted the Washingtonian Pledge. It still exists; and, in 1861, numbers two hundred and twelve members, most of whom are active, exemplary, temperance men and women. Who will criminate the citizens of

Litchfield township for the manner in which they celebrated 4th July, 1832?

In 1832 there was only one house at the Center, which was built and owned by George Olcott. The nearest house to the Center was that of Lewis Finley on the north, on the east that of D. Conyer, on the south that of W. Cole, on the west that of G. Pomeroy.

Mr. Shaler was the first Congregational preacher.

William Converse was the first physician.

Mr. Moses was the first tanner and shoe-maker, and in due course of time he became the first saddle and harness maker; and, still persevering, he became the builder and owner of the first steam grist-mill.

Asahel Howd was the first store-keeper.

The first female teacher was Almira Nickerson.

The first Congregational Church was formed in 1833, composed of twenty-two members. The same Church in 1861 numbers eighty members.

The first Baptist Church was established in August, 1833, with thirteen members. Rev. Asa Strait was the first pastor in that Church. The number of members increased to thirty-two; harmony prevailed; but in 1848, owing to causes that then prevailed, the church organization ceased.

The first Episcopal Methodist Class was formed in September, 1833, with ten members. It now numbers fifty-six members.

The first Protestant Methodist Class was formed in 1841, with six members. It now numbers, at least, forty members.

The second Baptist Church was organized in February, 1844, with sixteen members, and at present numbers about thirty members.

There is a strange incident relative to the sexes born in this township since its organization. The number of births is three hundred and seventy two in fifteen years, two hundred and ten of which are males and one hundred and sixty-two females. Should all tarry at home, and live to count three score and ten years, there is a strong probability that the year 1900 may find a full hundred of shrivelled old bachelors travelling solitary and alone within the precincts of the township.

There have been one hundred and four marriages within the township, up to 1845. Within fifteen years, one hundred and twenty-four persons have deceased in the township since the first death, being a fraction more than eight each year. If the number of deaths that occur can be relied on as an index of health, or the reverse, certainly the township of Litchfield may compare, in salubrity, with any other section of the county.

The oldest pioneer residing in the township is Charles Richards, who came in 1830. The next three entitled to that appellation are, Mrs. S. Strait, N. Strait, and J. V. Strait. To them there is a marked difference between what they saw in 1831, and what they see in 1861.

In 1832, when the Assessor travelled over the township to take a list of the property subject to taxation, he returned—one horse and twenty-four cattle, as appears on duplicate, valued at two hundred and thirty-two dollars. Compare that list with the number and value of horses and cattle in the annexed statistical table, and those of the first settlers; who examine, will hardly believe that so great an increase could be made in thirty years—a striking proof of what industry and economy can accomplish:

LITCHFIELD STATISTICS.

PERSONAL PROPERTY.	Number.	Value.
Horses,	478	$21,940
Cattle,	1,520	18,361
Sheep,	5,895	11,276
Hogs,	564	1,783
Wheat, bushels.	6,000	6,000
Corn, "	28,650	7,200
Butter, pounds,	55,900	5,600
Cheese, "	50,200	3,100
Total of yearly value,		$75,260

If to the foregoing be added the amount that yearly accrues from Oats, Clover-seed, Grass Seeds, Potatoes, Barley, Flax, Orchards and Gardens, it would augment the sum at least fifty thousand dollars, making the yearly products of the township to be one hundred and twenty-five thousand two hundred and sixty.

A striking evidence of what can be done where industry and economy are the aims of those who toil.

LAFAYETTE.

In 1830, the lands and chattels within the present township of Lafayette, were owned by Apollos Cook, T. B. Cook, Lucy Day, S. and T. Fowler, Elijah Hubbard, Lemuel Moffatt, Samuel Moffatt's heirs and Wm. N. Sill, comprising an area of sixteen thousand and fifty-one acres, on which they paid a tax of three hundred and thirty-one dollars.

From 1818, to 1832, the lands now in the township of Lafayette were listed and taxed as belonging to Westfield, to which it was attached. In 1832, the township was organized, and at the first election ten votes were given. The first township officers were as follows; Vivalda Wood, Alexander Barrett and Anson Bellamy, Trustees; Ephraim Harris, Township Clerk; Vivalda Wood, Treasurer; and Vivalda Wood, Supervisor; Abraham Brooks, Justice of the Peace. As office timber was rather scarce, the voters, in their sovereign capacity, imposed upon Vivalda Wood the duties of three offices. At the election, the propriety of electing a Constable was duly considered and vetoed. It was then thought that collections could be made by Abraham alone.

As the number of votes, at the first election, require only a small space they are here given: William Bissett, David Ransom, Ezekiel Slater, Anson Bellamy, Henry F. Hall, Henry C. Ransom, Vivalda Wood, Alexander Barrett, Epraim Harris and Edward Starr, who may be considered as first settlers.

On April 17, 1824, Rev. Joel Goodell, by invitation, preached in a school house near Isaiah Doanes and organised the first Congregational Church. The following are the names of the first founders of the church: Abraham Brooks and Asenath Brooks, Ira Brooks and Fanny Brooks, Peter Brooks, Tabitha Brooks, Roswell Williams and Martha Lucas, Jerremiah Doty and Susan Doty, Matthew Leffingwell and Eveline Leffingwell, George Wallace and Emelia Doty, Milo Loomis and Lucy A. Loomis and Rozetta Doane.

In 1835. Rev. Kellum, of the Mothodist Episcopal Church, preached in the township and organized a class. The number of persons, and names, who formed that class are unknown.

In the same year the Baptist Church was organized but with what number is now unknown.

In 1838, the Disciples Church was established and had a goodly number of members at commencement.

In 1843, the United Brethren organized a church to which accessions, not a few, have been added.

In the east part of the township the Presbyterians have a church erected and quite a number of members.

If churches are an index of a prevalent moral and religious sentiment, there is no township of the same age in the county, that has exhibited greater benevolence in contributing to, and erecting churches than Lafayette.

In wealth or natural facilities they will not claim greater advantages than other townships, yet in the erection of churches they have shown a liberality that every observer must commend.

Before the township was ten years organized the citizens of the different christian denominations have, with the aid of other benevolent residents within and near to the township, erected the following church edifices at the probable cost given; Congregational Church, two thousand and two hundred dollars; Episcopal Methodist, one thousand and three hundred dollars; Baptist, one thousand and three hundred dollars; Disciples, one thousand and two hundred dollars; United Brethren, one thousand dollars; Presbyterian, one thousand dollars.

Each church has a membership of not less than fifty-five, and the whole combined may be acknowledged to sustain a reformatory influence over the inhabitants of the township.

It is worthy of record that actions at law have never been numerous or of long and angry continuance between the inhabitants of the township, and when men from there are seen in court they are more frequently jurors than parties in actions.

The township is rapidly filling with sober, industrious, economical farmers and mechanics who delight in making home their choice resort; and the arrangement of the farms, the neat and properly arranged dwellings and barns, and the choice kind of fruit in their orchards give evidence of good taste, and industrious applications.

In 1820, S. and J. Fowler owned four thousand and six hundred acres in the township, on which they, in that year, paid a tax of thirty-four dollars and forty-five cents. Those among whom that body of land has been subdivided and now owned, can form some estimate of the then value and contrast present advantages and facilities with those that owners then enjoyed.

LIVERPOOL STATISTICS.

PERSONAL PROPERTY.	Number.	Value.
Horses,	551	$23,459
Cattle,	1,648	17,640
Sheep,	9,199	12,180
Hogs,	847	2,520
Carriages and Wagons,	121	3,980
Moneys and Credits,		34,900
Butter, pounds,	53,710	5,370
Cheese, "	35,780	2,380
Wheat, bushels,	11,412	11,412
Corn, "	34,760	8,490
Yearly product as listed in 1681,		$123,251

If to the foregoing be added the surplus that yearly accrues from the products of oats, clover-seed, grass-seed, potatoes, orchards and gardens, it is safe to say that the yearly products of the township amounts to one hundred and sixty three thousand dollars.

Compare 1832, with 1861, and how marked the progress in value, in improvements and in productions.

MEDINA.

The principal proprietor of this township was Hon. Elijah Boardman, of New Milford, Connecticut. He was born March 7, 1760. In 1776, he enlisted as a common soldier, was taken very sick at New York, and was removed to Kingsbridge.

Providentially was found by a neighbor of his father, who took him to a place of safety, gave notice of his situation, when his father immediately came to his relief.

In 1795, Mr. Boardman became a member of the Connecticut land company, and a very considerable amount of land in the Western Reserve fell into his hands.

Homer Boardman, Judson Canfield, Zepheniah Briggs and Roger Skinner were also proprietors of a few lots in Medina.

Mr. Boardman had become a man of some prominence in Connecticut; was elected six times a member of the State Legislature. In 1819, was elected State Senator, and in 1821, Senator of the United States. He occupied his seat during the two sessions of the seventeenth Congress, and having been elected for six years, was a member at the time of his death, which occurred in 1823, at Boardman, Ohio.

Medina was surveyed into lots, eighty-one in number, in 1810. The first cabin was erected by a Mr. Hinman and brothers on lot Twenty-two. They chopped about three acres, remained a short time, and for fear of the Indians left and never returned; they were said to have been from Aurora. Zenas Hamilton was the first actual settler. He was born in Danbury, Connecticut, November 6, 1781, removed from there to Harpersfield, New York, remained there one year and a half, and as he had previously made a purchase of some land in Medina, he accordingly pursued his journey and arrived with his family October 3, 1814, and went into the lone cabin aforesaid, being hardly a shelter for them until he could roll up another near by, on lot Twenty-two, being a part of his purchase. Mr. Hamilton, with his family of seven or eight in number, were alone for a year and a half, before any other family arrived. They had to fare as best they could. Sometimes they would put corn into a small leathern bag and pound upon the head of an axe, and again shell out wheat and rye by hand and boil it and supply their wants until they could get from the mill twenty or more miles distant. Their trials and privations must be experienced to be realized. Mr. Hamilton had the good fortune to kill a bear almost the first thing after his arrival. During the first few years he killed fifteen bears, besides a great number of deer and turkies.

In consequence of his being so fortunate and efficient in hunting, they were pretty well supplied with meat. There pioneers were provided for; the meat of the bear was much like pork, quite palatable to a woodman. The meat of the deer and turkies was somewhat drier than beef or the domestic fowl but we were thankful for it, and surely had no reason to complain. Mr. Hamilton, at one time, as he approached a large oak tree, discovered a large bear at the foot, eating acorns, and as he looked up he saw the old one with two cubs getting off the acorns. Knowing that those on the tree would come down as soon as he fired at the one on the ground, he prepared himself by taking some bullets in his mouth so that he could load his rifle quick, and immediately shot the larger one at the foot of the tree, then put some powder into his gun, spit a ball in and gave it a chunk on the ground, when it would prime itself, and in that way shot the others before they could get down, and thus had them all but one, in a heap, in a very short time.

Mr. Hamilton had no cow until the next harvest time after his arrival, when he bought one in Columbia and brought her home to the great joy of the children.

NARRATIVE OF JAMES MOORE.

In my early life the old song "And well settled on the bank of the pleasant Ohio," had something to do in what afterwards became a settled purpose, and in company with a young man about to settle in West Bloomfield, New York, started, January 1, 1816, from Boston, Massachusetts, on runners, snow about one and a half feet deep. In passing the Green Mountains, in Vermont, we tarried over night at Mr. Strong's, the agent for Strongsville, Cuyahoga county, Ohio, and in part the agent to survey what was afterwards the township of Strongsville. We pursued our journey, and arrived in West Bloomfield about the last of June, where my horse failed me. I took a seat in the mail stage to Buffalo, from thence to Cleveland by private conveyance. At this time no stage run on the lake shore road; in fact, there was little or no road; yet the wilderness was full of emigrants going west, who had been pent up by the three years war. We arrived in Cleveland the fore part of March, 1816, where I found

Mr. Strong, the agent. At this time Cleveland contained but six or seven frame buildings. Munson and Shephard were keepers of public houses. Carter in the red house on the river bottom, kept the ferry; Dr. Long had an apothecary shop on main street.

The day following, Mr. Strong and party, with myself, I think all on foot, with such things as were absolutely necessary, started for Strongsville, where we arrived in season to build a good camp fire, and spent the night in a most primitive manner. The day after we spent, in rain and snow, in finding our way to Timothy Doan's in Columbia, where provisions were procured. We returned and spent several days in running lines; but finding that whenever I selected a lot it was reserved, I made the best excuse I could, and left for Mr. Doan's, and soon became acquainted with Captain Seymour, who volunteered to show me the Mill Site, where he and Mr. Doan would soon erect Mills in the Township of Medina. Accordingly the Captain, with tin cup, rifle, and most formidable butcher knife, led the way, and, as if by instinct, found his way some ten or eleven miles through a dense forest. After viewing the Mill Site, we descended the branch of Rocky River, as far as lot fifty-two, and after some examination, found our way to Zenas Hamilton, where we spent the night. In the morning the Beach Tree, conspicuous as the seat of justice of Medina county, was visited; and if size gives importance, this tree was truly important. It stood some forty or fifty feet a little north of east in front of the old Court House. At this time about the 20th of March, 1816, Zenas Hamilton was the only inhabitant in the township. While I was getting materials together on lot fifty-two for a cabin, James Palmer, Chamberlin and Marsh arrived and assisted me in putting up my cabin, being the third in the township; this must have been in the fore part of April, 1816. I cut and cleared, without team, three acres where David Nettleton's house now stands, and planted it with corn, and left in care of Joab Marsh. The last of May, 1816, I started for Boston, and returned in October of the same year. During my absence, several cabins were erected. In April, 1816, Mr. Hulet, in the west part of Brunswick, was, after Z. Hamilton, my nearest neighbor in that direction, and Mr. Mott east on the old Smith road, each about seven miles from my cabin. Our nearest post-office was Cleveland. Pork was then thirty dollars per barrel, tea one dollar and fifty cents per pound, wheat one dollar and fifty cents per bushel, corn and potatoes one dollar per bushel each, tobacco and sole leather fifty cents per pound, eight-penny nails twenty-five cents per pound, &c.

Chamberlin and Marsh remained in Medina but a short time, and moved to Sullivan. James Palmer put up his cabin on lot sixteen, and improved it, and made himself a good farm, with every needed convenience, and remained on it until his death, which occurred in February, 1850. He was a very upright, worthy citizen; much esteemed by all who knew him. Mr. More's family arrived with Mr. Andrew Seaton and family from Boston in 1818. Mr. Seaton died in the summer of 1826. Mr. More remained on lot fifty-two until 1828 or 1829, when he went on to lot seventy-three, and erected a good house in company with Nathan Northrop, cleared up the farm, and added all needed buildings, with good fruit, all in good state of cultivation. In 1832 they sold out to Daniel Northrop. Mr. Moore, in company with Erastus Luce, purchased a farm in the north-west part of Medina, near Abbeyville, built a splendid mansion, made many important improvemts, and in a few years sold out again. Mr. Moore removed to Lake county, Illinois, where he still resides. He was a man of more than ordinary ability; honest, prompt, and persevering in every engagement; in a word, a kind-hearted and very worthy citizen.

On the 11th day of June, 1816, Rufus Ferris, Esq., arrived with his family; and, having a number of hands in his employ, soon erected a shanty for their things, and did their working by the side of a fallen tree. Mrs. Ferris had to bake every day, rain or shine. He soon erected a log house, half a mile north of the Public Square in Medina. He was agent for Mr. Boardman, and his house was open and free for all who came to purchase land in the township. He, with his men, pushed forward the chopping and clearing as fast as they could, and soon had corn and wheat growing on the ground so recently an entire wilderness. They were formerly from New Milford, Connecticut.

In the fall of 1816, a number of lots were selected by different individuals. In October, Noah M. Bronson and Noah Warner, from Plymouth, Connecticut, made purchase of lots thirty-seven, fifty-four and fifty-five; and about the same time, Noice B. and Dathan Northrop, from Cornwall, Connecticut, after spending a day and a night in the woods, and then changing their course, succeeded in finding their way to Ferris' cabin, thankful for a dish of potatoes and venison, after having fasted thirty odd hours. They selected lots thirty and fifty-six. Seth Roberts was with them.

In November, 1816, Dathan Northrop came on and put up the logs and roof of a cabin for Joseph Northrop and family, who had stopped in Nelson, Portage county, and waited for sledding until the last of January, 1817, when they removed to Medina and went in with Esq. Ferris. There they remained until they could mud up the cabin. In order to do this they had to heat water, and dig through the snow then eight inches deep. This being accomplished, they moved into it the 6th day of February, 1817, without door, floor, or chimney. The weather was very cold, but plenty of wood at hand, and they were quite comfortable, and thankful. In a few days, built a stick chimney, hewed puncheon boards for door and table. Pole bedsteads and stools or benches constituted the furniture for the time being.

All the pioneers for the first year had to suffer more or less for the want of bread and potatoes, in consequence of the distance to where they could be obtained. N. B. Northrop went fifteen miles in the spring, paid ten dollars for twenty bushels of potatoes, and five dollars to get them hauled in. He had previously been twenty miles for the first load of wheat, paid one dollar and fifty cents per bushel, got it ground, and paid a like sum to get it home. Also paid three dollars for the first bushel of salt, thirty-four dollars and fifty cents for the first cow, twenty-six dollars for the first barrel of pork and three calf heads, and poor at that. F. A. Abbott and N. B. Northrop paid eleven dollars for a barrel of Liverpool salt, and it fell short one-tenth. All this don't begin to tell the story of many of the pioneers of these then new settlements. The multitude of comforts, nuts, fruits, &c., which are now usually abundant, we did not then expect or hope for. But by the blessing of a good, kind Providence we have many of us lived to realize more than our most sanguine expectations.

It was on the 11th day of March, 1817, that the first public religious service was ever conducted in this then wilderness township. Sermon by Rev. Royce Searl,

Rector of St. Peter's Church, Plymouth, Connecticut. Services the next day also; sermon by Rev. William Hanford, Missionary from Connecticut. Both at the house of Zenas Hamilton. Some time after, Mr. Searl organized St. Paul's Parish, of Medina. The following names are on the original record, viz: Rufus Ferris, Miles Seymour, Benjamin Hull, Harvey Hickox, David Warner, William Painter, George Warner, Mirah B. Welton, and Zenas Hamilton. All the above-named persons have since died or removed.

In early spring of 1817, William Painter, David and George Warner, from Plymouth, Connecticut, Lathrop Seymour, Timothy Doan and Samuel Y. Potter, from Columbia, and Isaac Barnes, Mr. Calender and some others, now became actual settlers.

In June, 1817, Esq. Ferris employed John Northrop and N. B. Northrop to hew the timber and frame the first barn built in Medina; it being also the first barn frame that N. B. Northrop had ever superintended as master workman. The timber being green and heavy, help was at that time necessarily obtained, in part, from Liverpool and Brunswick; and, not being able to complete the raising the first day, all had to lie over until morning. Ferris being fond of fun, prepared two large pails of milk-punch, sweet, but strong with whiskey; and in a short time six or eight of those who drank most freely were on their backs feeling upwards for terra firma. The raising was finished in the morning. Rufus, the youngest son of Esq. Ferris, now living in Lafayette, (though then a small boy,) says he well remembers that when the rafters and ridge-pole were up, Uncle John Hickox (as he was called) went up on the end rafter and walked the ridge-pole to the other end and down again to the plate. The barn is still standing now in 1861, being the same in which the first Court was held in and for Medina county.

The wife of Lathrop Seymour, (now widow Bradford,) presents the following Pioneer History, viz: That on the 20th day of September, 1807, they started from Waterbury, Connecticut, for the Western Reserve, in company with four other families, with ox-team, through mud and mired, to Buffalo; and that they took passage in a little dirty schooner; that they went ashore on Canada side and staid over Sunday at an old neighbors. They then went on board again, and in three weeks landed at Erie, Pennsylvania. Mr. Seymour and wife concluded not to go on board again, and Mr. Seymour started for Euclid. Mrs. Seymour, with Mr. Bromon, wife and child, commenced their journey on foot. Mrs. Seymour having been sick the three weeks they were on the schooner, she could walk only six miles in a day. Mr. Seymour arrived in Euclid the 14th of November, procured two horses and met them forty miles from Erie; they then completed their journey to Euclid on horseback. They remained there through the winter, went to Cleveland in the spring; stayed there three months; from thence they moved to Columbia, with the ague, which held on about nine months; during the time they lost their child. From thence they moved to Tallmage, where Mr. Seymour built a saw-mill. They again returned to Columbia, occupying their farm for a time; then went to Huron, where Mr. Seymour built another saw-mill. Again they returned to Columbia. War having been declared, they were in constant fear. Mr. Seymour being in the service, Mrs. Seymour was alone most of the time with her children, with trouble without and fears within. After a while the soldiers were stationed at home; and put up a block house, to which, at any alarm, they repaired for safety. Mrs. Seymour says that one night about twelve o'clock they had news that the British and Indians were landing at Huron; that they all got up, packed up their things and started for Portage county; that they had not got over ten miles when they camped out in the woods; that news came to them in the night more favorable, and in the morning they returned home. This was in the spring. She says that in September, after Perry's Victory, there was great rejoicing on the frontiers; they then commenced working on their farms. In 1814 they removed to Liverpool and boarded the hands that worked in the salt works. They were there a year, and went again to Columbia, from whence Captain Seymour came to Medina, in March, 1816, with James Moore, to view a mill-seat, which Doan and Seymour had previously purchased. They moved to Medina, April, 1817. They went into a little log shanty so small that when they camped down the floor was covered with their beds. The snakes were so thick that they were afraid of having a new bed-fellow before morning; they would stick their heads up through the floor and crawl on to their door-steps to sun.

Seymour and Doan erected a saw-mill in the fall of 1817. Grist-mills were at Middlebury and Stow, a four days' journey with oxen. Mrs. Seymour says that they once went three weeks without bread, living upon potatoes, meat and milk.

In 1818 Seymour and Doan built a grist-mill adjoining the saw-mill in Weymouth. Mrs. Seymour is now in her seventy-fifth year, and has been the mother of seven children, but two of whom are now living. She says it may be her life has been spared for greater trials, but God's will be done; and she further says that whatever the Lord may see fit to place upon her she will try to bear patiently. Captain Lathrop Seymour died December 19th, 1835.

On the tenth day of April, 1817, the people assembled, with teams and tools, at the place appointed, near the present residence of Chauncey Blakslee, cleared away the under-brush, cut the timber, hauled it together and put up a log meeting-house; cut the tree, made the shingles, covered it, etc. About noon notice came that Mr. Searl would be there and preach a sermon at four o'clock in the after-noon, that day. We did our best to be ready. We prepared seats by placing poles between the logs and stakes drove in the ground, and had it all ready in due time. Mr. Searl came and fulfilled his appointment. Nearly all were present who could get there. The exercises were accompanied with appropriate singing, and all passed off in very pleasant pioneer style.

The first school ever taught in Medina, was by Eliza Northrop, in the house above mentioned, in the summer of 1817. The names of the pupils were Joseph, Ruth, Elizabeth and Mary Hamilton; George, Lucius, Carlos and Lester Barnes; Banner and Harrison Seymour; Jared and Mary Doan; Anna, Cynthia, Philemon, Chloe, Ruth and Madison Rice; Clement and Freeman Marsh; Frank and Philander Calender; and Lois and Liusa Palmer: twenty-three.

Ruth and Elizabeth Hamilton, (now Mrs. Graham and Nettleton) and Harrison Seymour, are all that now remain in town of those first scholars that attended the first school ever taught in this, then wilderness, township.

The first person born was Matthew, son of Zenas Hamilton, June 9, 1815. He studied medicine, went West and was doing a good business as a practical physician, and in crossing a river to see a patient was drowned.

The first girl born was Eliza Sargent, August, 1818, now Mrs. Judge Humphreville, of Medina Village.

The first death was that of a young daughter of Asahel Parmaly, from Vermont, while stopping on their way to Sullivan. It occurred early in the spring of 1817.

On May 8, 1817, Ransom Clark, with his brother John L. Clark, arrived and purchased a part of lot Forty-five, and slept under their wagon, with elm bark for floor and siding, until they could build a shanty of such poles as they could handle themselves, with bark floor and ceiling. There they kept bachelor's hall through the summer. Ransom worked at his trade (joiner) in Wooster, through the winter, and John L. taught school in Columbia.

In June, 1718, F. A. Albert, with his family, arrived and soon after settled on lot Fifty-three, north half, and Agustus Phillips on the south half of the same lot. His father and mother came in 1820; they were colored people, descendants of King Phillips of ancient renown.

In June, 1817, James Warner and Gad Blakslee came from Plymouth, Connecticut, and located the central lot in Medina. In October following, E. A. Warner arrived and proceeded to put up a log house for his father's family, and to procure provisions and make such preparations as he could for their arrival, which occurred February 18, 1818. They went into their house in an unfinished state, as many others had to do in those days. Mr. Blakslee did not move in until some time after; he died some years since. James Warner is in his eighty-sixth year and smart, enjoying comfortable health.

In April, 1818, Dr. Bela B. Clark, a brother of Ransom and John L. Clark, arrived and informed them

MEDINA. 183

that their father, ⬤ Clark, was coming, and they left their chopping ⬤ cut the logs for a shanty for the family, and had got it up and three-fourths of the roof on when their father's team appeared in sight. They soon finished the roof, and the family crossed the river on flood ⬤ (the river being so high they could not cross th ⬤ th their teams) and carried their bedticks, (filling them with straw and leaves) and such other articles as they could, lodged in their cabins in real pioneer style, and like others of their neighbors before them, fared as best they could, They were forty days on their journey from Bridgewater Connecticut, arrived in June, 1818. The remaining Indians had had their camps along on Rocky river and vicinity, for a few of the first years; they were friendly, but incessant beggars. If rightly informed they left after the following manner; Mr. Hulett, of Brunswick, was at Nelson, Portage county, and saying something about the Indians being a nuisance, Captain D. Mills, the old pioneer hunter, well known to the Indians, told Mr. Hulett, that if he would tell them that Mills, Redding and some others that he named, was coming out there, and would make way with every Indian they could find he thought they would leave. Mr. Hulett did so, and sure enough, they packed their horses and left, and never returned.

ORGANIZATION.

By order of the commissioners of Portage county, dated March 24, 1818, the first election of township officers for Medina, was held the first Monday of April (6th day,) 1818. It was then organized by appointing Isaac Barnes, Noah M. Bronson and Abraham Scott,

MEDINA.

Judges; and Samuel Y. Potter ▓▓ of election. After being duly sworn, it was v▓▓▓hat Isaac Barnes be Township Clerk; Joseph Northrop, Abraham Scott and Timothy Doan, Trustees; Rufus Ferris and Lothrop Seymour, Overseers of the Poor; Abijah Marsh and Benjamine Hull, Fence V▓▓▓; James Palmer, Lister; Rufus Ferris, James ▓▓▓, Zenas Hamilton and William Painter, Supervisors; Samuel Y. Potter and Ransom Clark, Constables; and James Moore, Treasurer.

Ransom Clark is the only one living in Medina of all the first officers. James Moore is still living in Illinois; the others are all dead.

The first suit was nearly as follows: Joseph Northrop had bought a pig of a Mr. Woodward, of Bath. As the money was not sent quite as soon as Woodward expected, he sent his claim (two dollars) to Zenas Hamilton, Esq., the first Justice of the Peace, with orders for him to sue it. But Esq. Hamilton, rather than send a summons, went two miles through the woods, informed Mr. Northrop of the fact, and told him that if he would say that the money should be in hand three months from that time, he would do no more about it; and the matter ended. Justices in those days were frequently much more ready to save their neighbors trouble and expense, than to pocket their fees themselves.

The first couple married, were Giles Barnes and Eliza Northrop, on the 22d day of March, 1818. Rev. Royce Searl (Episcopal Clergyman) solemnized the marriage ceremony, after the Congregational form. Invitations were sent out for all the inhabitants of the township to attend the wedding. They held on rather late, but, as the boys had procured a dead load of torch bark, all were amply supplied, and went to their homes with torch in hand. Some were thought to be a little snapped with wine—(no, whiskey;)—but this was not considered very extraordinary, (even for some Clergymen,) under such circumstances, in those days.

The first Congregational Church was organized February 21st, 1819, by Rev. William Hanford, Missionary from Connecticut, assisted by Rev. Simeon Woodruff. The Church was organized at the house of Isaac Barnes, and consisted of seven members, viz: Joseph Northrop, Charity Northrop, Isaac Barnes, Marther Barnes, Nira B. Northrop, Giles Barnes and John Barnes. All have died except Nira B. Northrop and Giles Barnes. Mr. Hanford, Missionary, occasionally preached in Medina, for four or five years. Joseph Northrop was born in Brookfield, Connecticut, June 13th, 1766; Charity, his wife, was born in Stratford, Connecticut, February 6th, 1769. They removed from Brookfield to Cornwall, Connecticut, February, 1796, and from thence to Medina, as before mentioned, when there were but two families in the township; but several others arrived soon after. Joseph Northrop first settled on the bank of Rocky River, north side of the east and west road, lot thirty. After seven years, he moved on to lot fifty-six, where he remained until his death, which occurred July 21st, 1843, in the seventy-eighth year of his age. Charity, his wife, died December 26th, 1851, in the eighty-third year of her age. Isaac and Marther Barnes were from Camden, New York, and, after ten or twelve years, removed to Richland, Kalamazoo county, Michigan, and have since both died. Nira B. Northrop was born in Brookfield, Connecticut, December 8th, 1791, and still lives, on lot fifty-six, the same he bought in 1816. Giles and John Barns were from West Hartford, Connecticut. Giles now lives in Weymouth. John went to Hudson, first, from here, and thence to Richland, Michigan, and has recently died. Life is as a vapor; it appeareth for a short season, and then vanisheth away.

The Episcopal Methodists held meetings early, in the village of Medina, perhaps in 1819 or 1820; but the record is not to be found, as yet. The Baptist and Free Will Baptist Churches were organized some time after 1830 and 1840; the United Brethren in Christ also about 1859. The exact dates have not been obtained.

One goeth and another cometh, improvements still progressing. In 1818, Moore & Stevenson erected a saw-mill in Bagdad. James Warner soon purchased the mill and privilege, and with his son-in-law, Steven N. Sargent, erected a grist-mill in 1820, just below the saw-mill.

Early in 1818, Noah M. Bronson moved his family and settled on the lot (thirty-seven) that he purchased in 1816. He had resided in Ashtabula for some time previous. He was, for a number of years, Associate Judge in the Court of Common Pleas, in Medina county, and lived on his farm to the advanced age of ninety-two years.

In 1818, David Allen, John Briggs, Selden B. Welton, Eden Hamilton, Esq., and their families arrived. Arza, Lindley, and Eden Hamilton, jr., Jacob R. Welton and David Nettleton, were permanent settlers. Several others also came, and remained a few years, and have gone West.

Religious meetings were conducted on the Sabbath, in the house erected April 10th, 1817, during the season; one-half of the day by the Episcopalians, and the other by the Congregationalists. Soon after, a log house was built at the Center, where meetings were continued harmoniously until the house was burned.

The people built a town-house, where Episcopal service was conducted until that was also burned. The Congregational people built a meeting-house at Bagdad, and met there and at the village alternately, for a number of years. Rev. Lot B. Sullivan was the first minister of the Congregational Church, for one year, one-half of the time; the other half in Wellington. Rev. Horace Smith was with Medina and Granger six months, as a Missionary, sent by the Hampshire Missionary Society, Massachusetts. Rev. S. V. Barnes came in 1827, by the aid of Aristarchus Champion, Esq., of Rochester, New York. His labors were abundant, resulting in a general revival in the east part of the township, and afterwards in the village and vicinity. He was the stated minister in Medina and Weymouth for a number of years. Religious, moral and temperance reform were gaining the ascendency; schools were improving; and every important enterprise was cherished, and urged onward to success. Thus we seemed to see the wilderness and solitary place literally budding and blossoming as the rose, and indeed becoming vocal with the praises of the Most High God.

The first sudden death occurred at the raising of a log barn for Giles Barnes, on lot seventy-one, August 12th, 1819. Isaac J. Pond was instantly killed as he was taking up a rafter, standing on the north-east corner. The butting pole rolled, and he, losing his balance, jumped on to the ground, and as he was endeavoring to rise upon his feet, the rafter struck him across the temple. I sprang to him, and no sooner than I reached him the blood poured forth from his nose and mouth, and he died without moving a finger.

His wife, though fainting at the first intelligence, soon became composed, and in the exercise of Christian fortitude was enabled to bear the affliction as well as any woman under such circumstances. Their little son, Henry N. Pond, was just three months old that day. Mrs. Pond had the sympathy of every member of the community. The remains of the deceased were interred the next day, a little west of the then residence of F. A. Abbott, on lot fifty-three.

I will mention here that not far from thirty years from that time, the same Henry N. Pond, who had for some time been the head of a family, while at work in his field was instantly killed by the fall of a dead tree. Both father and son were much respected and worthy citizens; and in both cases the whole people deeply mourned their loss. The widows of both father and son are still living, and have each, several years since, buried a second husband. As the changing seasons roll on, so does the sunny and shady side of this mortal life appear.

ANECDOTES.

In 1820, Harmon Munson, aged eighty-two, and wife, Johnson Warner and Joseph Pritchard and families arrived and settled near the center. About the first court after Mr. Munson arrived, he thought he would attend. He being so much older than any body else, of course attracted considerable attention. As he seated himself in Esq. Hickox's tavern, Judge Todd approached him and enquired where he was from, etc. Mr. Munson, without knowing that the person was Judge Todd, told him that he thought he would come and see the Judge and lawyers and get acquainted, and remarked that he supposed the Judge had not arrived yet. Yes, says the Judge he is here. Mr. Munson says, I understand he is a pretty smart man. Smart enough, says the Judge. But, says Munson, they say he drinks. The Judge's reply I have not learned. At any rate he wished the people to call him George Todd, except when he was in the Judge's seat.

During the time of the Rectorship of Mr. Searle, in connection with St. Paul's Church in Medina, a somewhat exciting difficulty occurred among some of the members, and at the same time the Episcopal Methodists at the village manifested considerable engagedness in their prayer meetings, and in reply to some remarks of Esq. Ferris, upon the subject, Seth Roberts said that the d——l had really come to Medina, had got the Episcopalians all by the ears, and frightened the Methodists to their prayers; and the
   Presbyterians look on and sing,
   Sweet is the work my God and King.

At a certain time a lady had been repeatedly abused and her life threatened by her husband when intoxicated, and to that degree, that she went before a Justice of the Peace and swore the peace against him. He was offered bail for his future good behavior, but refused to take it; accordingly the Court made a mittimus ordering the constable to take him to jail; and on this, he requested the privilege of stopping at his house, which being granted, he took a bag and put in one end his gallon bottle of whiskey, and in the other the large family Bible, placed them across his saddle; and thus took them with him to jail. In a few weeks he was bailed out, none the worse for having spent a short time there.

About this time the wolves began to commit their depredations. Mr. Gad Blakeslee had procured a fine flock of sheep, and the wolves killed eighteen at one time. It was found that they inhabited the wind-fall, in the south part of the township. They got Zenas Hamilton to go and assist in building a dead-fall, in which, together with a large steel-trap, they caught nine old wolves, (and ten to carry) and one more old one the next year. There has been but one known to have been seen in these parts since.

Burrit Blakeslee caught several otters about Rocky River during the first few years of the settlement.

N. B. NORTHROP'S HUNTING STORY.

In October, 1821, as I was on my way home from Weymouth, passing a lot belonging to Friend Ives, (now Isaac Bronson's) near the road I saw a flock of wild turkeys of about fifty. As I was on horseback, they did not seem much alarmed. I called at the house, asked Mrs. Ives if Mr. Ives had got a gun and powder and shot. Being answered in the affirmative, I took the gun, an old queen's arm, very rusty. However, I loaded pretty heavy, put in a handful of coarse shot just right for the occasion, and as I went to the door I met Mr. Ives and H. Selkirk, I told them what I was about to do, which was to go down on the east side of the lot under cover of some bushes, behind which I should be undiscovered, and requested them to walk slowly up the road and moderately show themselves to the turkeys that they might come near me. But as I approached the lot behind the bush and fence, a large turkey says, quit, quit. I dropped down upon my knee, balancing my gun with my elbow upon my knee, and looking through the leaves I saw the large turkey about thirty feet from me and the rest moving along in range, when I pulled away at them, and laid six of them sprawling, and myself too, on my back, gun and hat beyond me. When I recovered from the shock and got over the fence, Messrs. Ives and Selkirk were picking up the turkeys. I gave each of them one and tied four to my saddle, and started for home, quite well satisfied, notwithstanding the hard thump from the old gun.

In May, 1818, a general hunt was organized, comprising the north-west part or quarter of Brunswick, the north-east quarter of Liverpool, the south-east quarter of Columbia and the south-west quarter of Strongsville. The lines were all formed, the march had proceeded for some distance when a large buck came up and broke the line near where Jeremiah Warner was passing on with the line. Esq. Hamilton says to him, why don't you shoot that buck? He then cocked his gun, but too late, he thought; and says that he must have been careless, for as he was uncocking his gun it went off and being on his arm, lengthwise of the line it was supposed that the ball struck a limb and glanced downward, struck William Pritchard, passing through his heart killing him instantly. This was done May 16, 1821, he would have been sixteen years old the 29th of the next month. The hunt was broken up, and there has been no occasion for the like since.

A BACK-WOODS CELEBRATION.

The anniversary of American Independence was celebrated at Medina, July 4, 1821, not by the ringing of church bells and firing of cannon, but by the rustling of leaves, singing of birds and tinkling of cow-bells. John Freeze presided, assisted by Dr. B. B.

Clark. The Declaration of Independence was read by A. G. Hickox, and an appropriate oration delivered by Rev. R. Searle. A sumptuous repast was served by the good wives, of which all partook thankfully and harmoniously. After the feasting was over, the following toasts were read and loudly cheered. Sweetened whiskey, a very essential beverage, was imbibed freely at the cheering of every toast, and was repeated when a response was given.

1. The 4th of July, 1821.—Forty-six years have passed away since the prize was won, and still the value of Independence increases.

2. The President and Vice President and Head of Departments of the United States.

3. The memory of George Washington. (Drank standing.)

4. The Constitution of the United States.—Its characteristic features are liberty and equality.

(Hail Columbia was sung by all.)

5. Adams, Jefferson, Madison.—Amiable in private and public life.

6. The State of Ohio.—Although a young sister of the Republic, yet her patriotic exertions in the last war will be remembered long.

7. The Spirit of Freedom. Its seeds are sowing.—May they take deep root, spring up and bring forth a hundred fold and utterly root out the thistles of tyranny and oppression.

Among the volunteer toasts then given and cheered, the following is selected:

By Captain Herman Munson (aged eighty-three.)—Freedom to the Africans.

MEDINA STATISTICS.

PERSONAL PROPERTY.	Number.	Value.
Horses,	443	$20,779
Cattle,	1,427	18,139
Sheep,	4,945	9,519
Hogs,	415	1,379
Carriages and Wagons,	224	5,499
Moneys and Credits,		14,553
Wheat, bushels,	2,186	2,650
Corn, "	27,120	5,143
Butter, pounds,	26,557	2,186
Cheese, "	87,394	6,780
Total value of Township,		$86,627

MEDINA VILLAGE STATISTICS.

PERSONAL PROPERTY.	Number.	Value.
Horses,	216	$12,100
Cattle,	266	4,185
Sheep,	538	1,248
Hogs,	128	381
Carriages and Wagons,	180	6,780
Merchants' Stock,		36,266
Manufacturers' Stock,		7,891
Moneys,		9,792
Book Accounts and Credits,		74,792
Total Value for Village,		$153,436
Total for Township and Village,		$240,063

MONTVILLE.

BY AUSTIN BADGER.

I was born, reared and educated in the State of New York, and during the war of 1812, I participated in the duties of the camp and had a full test of the many privations that are consequent upon a soldier's life. I witnessed many of the scenes that have now become part of the history of that war and tested fully the toils and troubles of a life in the tented field.

After the close of that war and the proclamation of peace, I came to the conclusion that my native State did not contain all the elbow room necessary for an ambition like my own, and came to the conclusion that in the western wilderness I might find an opening where I could, in future, enjoy a full share of life's comforts, without being circumscribed by a narrow bound.

In the month of April, I left my native State and came into Medina county in May, 1818. There was a striking contrast between the country I left, and that into which I had just entered. The openings made by the axe-men, were comparatively few; and the cabins built and occupied by the settlers were rudely constructed and far between. A view of the almost unbroken forest seemed to overcome resolution, and I sometimes feared lest my physical powers would give way before I could make an opening and erect a cabin. But when I saw what others had done, I resolved to purchase, open and rear me a home in Medina county. I built the first double log house on the same ground where

MONTVILLE.

Bronson's brick block now stands, and commenced keeping tavern in company with Hickox, who was a married man, I was then unmarried. The court was held in the upper story of our house. I erected a second cabin house on the same lot where stands the dwelling of William H. Canfield. In the year 1819, I cleared off, upon contract, what is now called the Public Square. In 1819, the 4th of July came, as it had come in former years, and it was resolved by the citizens who lived near, that it should be observed with appropriate honors. In the morning a long pole was cut and stuck in a hollow beach stump, where the old Court House now stands, and on its top streamed gloriously, and unrivalled in the air a bandanna handkerchief, being the best fac simile of the nation's flag, that could then be found and used.

Those who participated in that memorable celebration were A. Badger, R. Ferris, B. B. Clark, L. Seymour, T. Doan, S. Potter. R. Clark, Caleb Chase, Erastus Luce, Thomas Currier and perhaps some others. We drove forks in the ground, prongs upward; then laid on pole-stringers, then put on cross-ties and covered the whole top with peeled bark, on which we set our provisions and standing up around our hastily-rigged, and sumptuously piled table, discussed of past events, and the future prospects of our nation, our State and our county. Good whiskey being one of the necessary articles on such a day, was bountifully furnished and plentifully drank as a beverage. Sentimental toasts were drank and always responded to by three hearty yells, and as many drinks of liquor. Whiskey sweetened with home-made sugar constituted the drink that was handed around, in the fashionable circle, in those days. In the evening we returned to our cabins highly gratified with the glorious celebration of the nation's birth-day. We, on that day, gave names to all the streets, or main roads that then centered in the village, by which names they are still called.

In April, 1819, I settled in Montville township. Samuel Brown was then there, and is entitled to the appellation of first settler in Montville. Shortly after my commencement there, Parker Pelton, A. Smith and Thomas Currier, with their families, became residents. In 1820, great arrangements were made to celebrate the 4th of July in good style, and we all concluded to go. Every one who wished to participate, was notified to bring provisions with him. All the inhabitants of Montville attended that celebration, and let it be recorded as a part of history that on the 4th of July, 1820, no human being could be found in Montville township, for the reason that patriotism fired every inhabitant to be at the celebration. Three ox teams hauled to Medina, on that day every living soul in Montville township, together with a young fat hog, a fat sheep and a few chickens intended to be eaten in common at the great celebration. From every inhabited township in the county, the people came with their ox teams, and by noon there was a large gathering and a cordial greeting. The dinner was of the best that the country then afforded, and all fared plentifully. Sweetened liquor was made in a tub which was re-filled often during the day. From that tub every person dipped in a tin and drank, when inclination prompted. Many of the more sturdy men took the whiskey raw, saying that the sugar took away its flavor. That was considered a glorious day at the County Seat.

Montville township was organized in 1820. The first township Trustees were T. M. Currier, Aaron Smith and Austin Badger. G. F. Atherton, township Clerk. No Constable was elected, as the whole body of voters supposed there would not be any constable business to do. Philo Welton was elected Justice of the Peace; having received every vote but one. Ten votes were polled at the first election. At this period in the settlement of the township the following may be reckoned as first settlers: G. F. Atherton, Austin Badger, Samuel Brown, Thomas M. Currier, Aaron Smith, Seth Hoit. Parker Pelton, Amassa Smith, Joseph Pimlot and Philo Welton. At this stage of the onward progress to future wealth, there were two horses in the township, owned by A. Badger and Parker Pelton. In 1822 there were three horses and forty-one cattle in the township, as appears from the assessment made by Mr. Welton, to the County Auditor.

In 1824 Austin Badger was elected second Justice of the Peace. The votes then cast numbered fifteen, and was considered as strong evidence that the township was growing in population very rapidly.

The first marriage in the township was W. R. Williams to Nancy Monroe. Henry Pelton was the first child born in the township. The first death and burial in the township was Mrs. Catharine Badger. The first teacher was Caroline Babbitt, who trained the youthful minds of eight scholars, in the first school-house, erected on the corner of the farm of A. Badger. Parker Pelton raised the first three acres of wheat ever cut in the township, and Austin Badger threshed it out with a flail for the seventh bushel, and thought it a good chance, to pay for wheat on that condition. The first blacksmith was Parker Pelton, who acted in that station when necessary, and was of essential service to the community.

Rev. Alva Sanford organized a Parish, of the Episcopal order, in 1829, comprising nine members, which continued its existence up to the organization of the

Episcopal Church in Medina, of which it became a part. In 1830 the Methodists constituted a Class and erected a Church, which is still in existence.

The first frame house was erected by Mr. Welton, and the first frame barn by George F. Atherton. The lumber then used was sawed at Bagdad, and hauled through the woods, the teamster making his own road as he travelled. In those days Mr. Badger did not consider it an extraordinary effort to cut, score and haul the timber necessary for a barn or a house. The township now (1861) has six school-houses, two steam saw-mills, comfortable dwellings, commodious barns, well arranged farms, a full share of industrial improvements, and is rapidly increasing in population and wealth.

MONTVILLE STATISTICS.

PERSONAL PROPERTY.	Number.	Value.
Horses,	413	$20,667
Cattle,	1,458	15,545
Sheep,	6,639	14,481
Hogs,	662	2,196
Carriages and Wagons,	197	5,193
Moneys and Credits,		18,876
Butter,	49,385	4,939
Cheese,	63,575	2,150
Wheat,	8,600	8,600
Corn,	58,500	14,650
Total value,		$107,234

If to the foregoing be added the yearly wealth that accrues from the products of oats, clover-seed, grass-seed, potatoes, orchards and gardens, the annual value of the personal property and products are worth one hundred and forty-five thousand dollars.

Contrast 1820 with 1861, and the increase must bear full evidence that the agricultural march of Montville has been onward for forty-one years.

SHARON.

Barnabas Crane was born in Barkley, Bristol county, Massachusetts, April 22d, 1775. His father, Bernice Crane, was a soldier in Canada, during the French war, where he endured great hardships and privations in that northern climate. He was, not once, but often, forced to sleep, (if sleep it might be termed,) on the freezing earth, with nothing but a soldier's clothing to protect him from the drifting snows and chilling winds. On one occasion the back part of his head was so severely frozen as to leave a mark that he carried during life. He lived to the age of four score and five years, and his companion, Jemimah Crane, died at the age of one hundred years, one month and fifteen days; each a pattern of good deeds while living.

The subject of this memoir was one of six, (one of whom, William Crane, now eighty years, is still residing in Sharon,) whose average ages were eighty years.

Owing to debility in youth, he was partially unfitted for manual labor; and, having a good opportunity of becoming a scholar, under the educational and moral training of Rev. Thomas Andros, of the Congregational Church, he applied himself closely to study, and became, not only thorough in English, but also in Latin. At the age of sixteen he became a teacher by profession, and practiced that calling for many years. Although chained by profession to terra firma, still his inclination led him to seek for a life on the ocean, and in due course of time he went aboard of a vessel destined for the Indies, by way of Cape Horn. The vessel sprung a leak when on the eastern coast of South America, and was there abandoned by the crew. He returned home, and, watching for another sea-faring voyage, his wishes were again gratified, by going on board of a vessel as a common hand. By degrees he rose from the station of a common hand to that of commander, and next, to being part owner of the vessel. For many years he sailed, to the West Indies and other ports, where commerce seemed to invite; yet he never crossed the Atlantic. Upon his return from sea, after having been absent some months, he learned that his kind companion had died on the 7th of April, 1825, leaving a family of nine children, the eldest only nineteen years old. All desire to leave his young family ceased, and duty and affection prompted him to extend to them that aid which none but a parent can bestow. Therefore he remained a widower, and in company with his young family spent many years of pleasure.

In May, 1833, he removed to Sharon township, while it was still a wilderness, and settled down. Having long since lost all anxiety to travel, in search of some easy way to gain a livelihood, he willingly and profitably devoted his time and energies in opening up and improving a farm, and, by careful and proper culture, gaining a full share of the comforts of life. Having, in former years, tasted the advantages resulting from a thorough, practical education, he strenuously urged the formation and elevation of common schools, and schools of a higher order; fully convinced that they were the nurseries of Republican institutions, intelligence, morality and religion.

Contrary to the faith in which he had been reared, and the earnest remonstrances of many friends, he was a strong advocate of Jefferson's political views, and a firm supporter of his administration. Often would he repeat the saying of Jefferson—"that one class of men are not born with saddles on their backs, and another class booted and spurred, by the grace of God, to ride them."

Jackson's policy and administration were fully endorsed by him. He was often heard to say that "the iron will and determination of purpose that Jackson exhibited, were traits of character calculated to challenge the highest admiration."

In middle life he had joined the Congregational Church, and had been a consistent member until 1840, when, becoming convinced of the fullness of the grace of God, as revealed in the Bible, he united with the first Universalist Society in Sharon, continuing his membership with that body until his decease.

Although a sea-faring man, and commander for many years, his most intimate friends never heard him use profane or obscene language; or, when relating an anecdote, in which he often practiced, no words were used that could offend the moral or the religious taste. Moving in the society and in the times that he did, the use of spirituous liquor was generally practiced; yet he was at all times, and under all circumstances so fully master of his appetite that alcohol, not himself, was the servant. When among the young he always advocated total abstinence, and urged them to practice it; yet he was frank to acknowledge that, owing to his training for many years, the jacket was rather straight for him to always wear. Outliving most of his children, he died at the residence of his son, on the third day of May, 1860. In death, as in life, he was calm, hopeful, patient and resigned.

SHARON.

NARRATIVE BY G. A. ROOT.

For a number of years previous to its settlement, the township of Sharon, or "Hart & Mather's," as it was then called, was noted as a common hunting-ground for the settlers of surrounding townships. As there were no settlements in this township for a considerable time after those in townships adjoining, all kinds of wild game were here found in abundance, and furnished an inducement for the visits of numerous hunting parties.

This state of things continued uninterrupted until the arrival, in 1816, of Mr. David Point, who settled on the farm now owned by Jacob Rudesill, in the north-east corner of the township. The township at that time was called, after its proprietors, Hart & Mathers, a firm, the members of which lived in Saybrook, Connecticut. Mr. Point is a native of Orange county, New York, and was born in 1786. In 1814 his father moved to Bath, in Summit county, where Mr. Point married a daughter of John Dunbar, and removed to Sharon, as above stated. He yet resides near the scene of his early labors in the settlement of the township, having reared to manhood and womanhood a family of nine children, besides losing five others. During the first year of his stay in the township, Mr. Point, besides building his house, cleared six acres of land, and sowed the "girdlings" with grain.

The first marriage that took place in the township, was that of Joseph Willey to Melinda McFarlin, in 1829. They afterward moved to Porter county, Indiana, where Willey died, in 1856.

The first white male child born in Sharon was Stephen Green, in 1819. He now lives in Bath. The first white female child was a daughter to Mr. and Mrs.

SHARON.

Point, June 16th, 1818. She is now married to George Vaughn, and resides in Allen county, Indiana.

The first death that occurred among the whites in the township was in the family of Point. An infant child, five months old, was attacked by the whooping cough, and died at the end of four weeks. This occurred in 1822, before the township could boast of a physician. There was one in Wadsworth, however, and for him Mr. Point went, but for some reason the Doctor was so engaged otherwise that he could not attend. As there were no grave-yards located, at that time, in Sharon, the body was taken to Granger for interment. No funeral sermon was preached on this occasion; a few neighbors gathered—for there were but few—at the house, where a prayer was offered and hymn sung, before starting for the grave.

The educational interests of the township were early attended to. A school meeting was called and held at the house of Mr. Point. Those who attended were David Point, Abram Valland, Lyman Green and Charles McFarlin. It was then agreed to build a school-house on the site now occupied by "Link's Tavern." There was an objection to this, however, which was, that several years before, an Indian squaw had been buried on the identical spot where the school-house would stand, and "spooks" were as plenty in those days as at present. But this objection did not prevail, and the school-house was built. According to tradition, this house was somewhat better than those commonly built in those times, it having an upper floor, (made of split logs,) and much care being devoted in its construction to make it comfortable; and on the whole it would compare favorably with many of more modern construction. All things being now ready, the first school in the township of Sharon commenced under the charge of Mr. David Holmes. The following list of scholars answered to the calling of the roll during that term of school, commencing in the fall of the year 1822: William, Polly, Rhoda and Sally Valland; John, Orville, Esther. Moses, Reuben, Merina, Almina and Wilson McFarlin; Jane, Betsey and Marilla Point; Lyman, Orpha, Dexter and Asenath Green. Myron, Chester and Tracy Hills.

Of the students above named all but three are now living. Mr. Holmes was married, while living in Sharon, to Miss Codding; and, in 1840, moved to Michigan, where he died.

The Methodist Church in Sharon was organized in April, 1832. There were twelve members present at the time. James Wilson was appointed Pastor in Charge. The names of members were, Valentine Waltman, class leader; Achsah Waltman and daughter, Charles McFarlin, Irena McFarlin. Almira McFarlin, George Lowerman, Susan Lowerman. Polly Lowerman, Rabecca Smith, Harriet Skinner and Martha Moore. During the following summer their number was increased to thirty members; and their ministry by Rev. Lorenzo Bivens, who was placed upon the circuit. In 1842 this denomination became strong enough to build a house of worship at the Center of the township.

From 1822, to 1829, nothing of much importance transpired except the arrival of new settlers, from time to time, and among whom. in 1828, came Mr. Peter A. Moore, who has been, since that time, and up to the time of his death, which took place at Omaha City, New York, in November. 1859, one of Sharon's most influential citizens. In 1829, the township was surveyed by Mr. Moore and George W. White, of Trumbull county, and the name changed from "Hart and Mathers," to that of Gash. This was done at the suggestion of Mr. Moore, in honor of his native State in Scotland This name, however, was retained by the township for only three motnhs, when it was again altered for the one it now bears.

The organization of the township took place in April, 1831. About seventy-five votes were cast, the result of which was the election of Peter A. Moore, Samuel Hayden and Charles McFarlin, Trustees; Jacob Rudesill, Clerk; Colonel Luther Fitch, Treasurer; Jonathan Smith, Justice of the Peace; Mark Smith, Constable. Of these, but one (Mr. Rudesill) is now living in the township.

Sunday, June 3, 1833, an event occurred which caused much excitement in Sharon, and at the same time, set the terrible consequence of intemperance in plain view of its inhabitants.

John Bleaks, a resident of the township, was in the habit of getting drunk occasionally. It was customary for him to go to Granger-burgh for liquor. One evening he was seen returning from there, far along in the stages of intoxication. Four days having passed without his returning home, and his family growing concerned as to his whereabouts, search was instituted by the neighbors. For several days the woods were rambled through in vain, till, on Sunday, ten days after he was last seen alive, his body was discovered, with his jug of liquor beside it. From the position of the body it was thought that he was stooping over to drink from a little creek, when he lost his balance and fell, his face in the water, from which position, through drunkenness, he was unable to extricate himself. A coroner's jury was summoned and verdict returned as above. The body was buried on the land now owned by Erastus Bissell. Before the grave was filled up, Cyrus Taylor threw the jug of liquor in, which was buried with the body.

While the jury were convened over the body of Bleaks, an accident occurred which came near proving fatal. A large tree, near by, was blown down, the top of which struck the head of William High and fractured his skull in a serious manner. He recovered, however, eventually. He was seven years old at the time of the accident.

It was during the year 1833, that Wm. Woodward, John Woodward, Joseph Daykin, Joseph Brunskell, John Bell, James Pratt and others, together with their families, came from England and settled in what is now known as the English Settlement, two miles northeast of the center of the township. Most of them yet reside in Sharon and are among the wealthiest and most substantial of its citizens. Their farms are models of neatness and order, and are stocked with the best of cattle, horses, etc.

The first store-room was erected and replenished with the necessary store goods in the autumn of 1834, by Dr. John Burge.

Luther Fitch was the first post master, whose appointment bears date in 1833, when the post office was established.

The first tavern was opened and kept at the center in 1835, by Milo and Horace Gibbs.

The first physician was Dr. Andrew Armstrong, who after a stay of two years moved, and the place was filled by Dr. Beach.

In 1835, a charter was granted by the Legislature, to erect the Sharon Academy, which was consummated. Mr. John McGregor was the first teacher, under whose supervision the institution made commendable progress, and from then to the present, the Sharon Academy has continued to be a good educational nursery.

SHARON STATISTICS.

PERSONAL PROPERTY.	Number.	Value.
Horses,	557	$29,451
Cattle,	1,875	21,470
Mules,	16	1,160
Sheep,	8,141	14,621
Hogs,	726	2,651
Carriages and Wagons,	248	7,649
Merchandise,		3,500
Moneys and Credits,		13,750
Butter,	63,117	6,325
Cheese,	12,160	740
Wheat,	18,570	18,500
Corn,	37,260	9,315
Total value,		$129,332

If to the foregoing be added the amount that yearly accrues from the products of oats, potatoes, clover-seed, grass-seeds, orchards and gardens, it may safely be asserted that the annual wealth of Sharon township cannot be less than $158,000; a strong evidence that perseverance and economy have been strictly observed by those who toiled in the field and in the work-shop.

SPENCER.

The original proprietor of the township was Samuel Parkman, of Vermont, who resided in the county of Geauga, Ohio, about thirty-four years since.

The first settler in the township was John P. Marsh, in the spring of 1823.

The first couple married in the township were Samuel Falconer to Margaret Bissett, by B. Irvin, Justice of the Peace, in 1830.

The first person born in the township was Samuel Marsh, March 25, 1826.

The first person who died in the township was Stephen Harrington, in 1826.

William Bishop kept the first school in a log cabin on the farm of John P. Marsh. Elizabeth Bissett, Phineas Davis, Phillip Bezard and John Space, composed his school. Seven of those scholars are, in 1861, residents in the township.

Rev. H. O. Sheldon started the first Methodist Class, in 1827, with Ruth Bezard, Z. Harrington, Elizabeth Space, John Space and Phebe Goodwin, members.

The township was organized in 1832, when twenty-one votes were cast. Abel Wood, Phillip Bezard and John Park, were elected trustees; Henry Wood, Clerk; and Ira Cole, Treasurer. Samuel Sooy was the first Justice after the organization.

The township of Spencer formerly constituted a part of Lorain county, to which it remained attached until 1839. The first record that is found on the Duplicate of Medina county is in 1840.

The advance made in clearing off the forest and in the erection of neat dwellings indicate, that at least some parts of its territory must have been tamed from its original wildness prior to 1820. The first rudely constructed cabins are rapidly disappearing. The stumps of the sturdy trees of the forest are rotted, the advances made in agricultural improvements, and the herds that graze upon the tamed pasturage, tell that Spencer township must have existed more than thirty years.

Forty years since, it must have composed a part of a large plat of wilderness where the hunter delighted to roam, and where the wild game sheltered themselves. There are doubtless many incidents and many privations that the first settlers knew and endured that must remain unwritten, because the actors have, years since, ceased to live, and no man of historical inclination has penned them.

In respect to fertility, timber, water and other natural advantages, Spencer can appear favorably with other townships in the county. The zigzag course of the river, sluggishly flowing through a wide but fertile portion of the township, and, in season of heavy rains, inundating a large area of low land, may, to the hasty observer, create unfavorable impressions as to the probability of its ever becoming valuable; but in the course of twenty years hence, when internal improvements become the watch-word of the people, the channel of that same river may be straightened and widened, and the objection to its overflowing the lands cease to exist. It is not vain to prophecy such a result, and when that improvement is made, the price per acre of land will rise rapidly.

The township is dotted, at proper localities, with school house, sthat indicate the wish of the owners of the lands that the rising generations should be properly trained and educated.

Church edifices are erected that speak well for the taste and generosity of the citizens. Mechanics of different orders have opened shops, and make and manufacture articles in demand. "Spencer Mills" had, and continue to have commendable notoriety. The farmers have given evidence of their design to become skilled in their avocation, by the arrangements they make as to their fields, grains, grasses, implements of husbandry, and every other article that is calculated to give fertility to soil, or add to productiveness.

There was a year in past history when the township could only count a few settlers, few cattle, few facilities, and few necessaries. That year of trial is now gone, and its scenes only remembered by a few. The present generation are enjoying a prosperity that was gathered at the expense of much toil and many obstacles. A generous, hard laboring grand-parent hands over, without a murmur, what he gained, to his grand-children, with the wish that they will use it frugally and with gratitude.

SPENCER STATISTICS.

PERSONAL PROPERTY.	Number.	Value.
Horses,	544	$24,544
Cattle,	2,093	22,729
Sheep,	1,746	3,361
Hogs,	1,133	3,181
Carriages and Wagons,	173	5,886
Moneys and Credits,		27,990
Butter, pounds,	78,819	7,890
Cheese, "	198,112	11,800
Wheat, bushels,	12,911	12,911
Corn, "	48,412	12,103
Total value of Township,		$136,395

If to the foregoing be added the wealth that accrues from the products of oats, potatoes, grass, clover-seed, grass-seed, orchards and gardens, the yearly products of Spencer township may, with safety, be reported at one hundred and fifty-three thousand dollars.

How striking the contrast between the valuation given in 1832 and that given in 1861! Let the same perseverance and economy be practiced for a second twenty-nine years, as was in the past, and the annual productions of the township will count three hundred thousand dollars.

WADSWORTH.

BY GEORGE LYMAN.

The original proprietors of this township were Elijah Wadsworth, William Ely, and John Tappan, together with some small proprietors.

The first settlement in Wadsworth was on the 17th of March, 1816, by Daniel Dean and Oliver Durham. Benjamin Dean, son of Daniel Dean, arrived on the 1st of March, and assisted in cutting the first tree for the purpose of making improvements R. F. Warner and his brother, Daniel, both came in the same year. Dean and Durham were originally from Vermont. They stopped awhile in Canfield, Mahoning county. Here they became acquainted with Elijah Wadsworth, the proprietor of tract One, of whom they purchased, and were to have any lots they might choose. Mr. Dean, on crossing the east line of the township, and stopping on the first lot, immediately made his selection, saying, I will take this lot. The township had previously been divided into nine tracts, among the different proprietors. Numbers two, three, four and seven, were small tracts. Number five, the north-east quarter, was called the Tappan tract; number six, the Smith tract; number one, the Wadsworth tract; and number eight, the Ely tract. Number nine was owned by several proprietors.

In 1815 Salmon Warner and Henry C. Wright, Christian and John Everhard, Christopher and William Baron, and their families, arrived in the township. In

1816 there was quite an increase of inhabitants—Jacob Miller, Samuel M. Hayden, Frederick Brown, Joseph Loomis, Jacob and Adam Smith, Benjamin Simcox, William Ally, Daniel Ware and Samuel Blocker, with their families; and Sherman Loomis, Steward and William C. Richards and George Razor, single men; in 1817, George Lyman, with his family, Lemuel North, Gordon Hillard and Timothy Hudson, single;—these all settled in the east part of the township. In 1818, Augustus Mills and family, Philo French, Heman and Amos Hanchet, Ira and Ephraim Moody, came in. Within the next six years the whole of the township, except the south-west quarter, was taken up and settled on. The number of inhabitants had increased to about nine hundred.

The first school was taught by Harriet Warner, in 1816. It was kept in one end of her father's log house, which, as was customary in those days, was built double. Among the scholars were Moses, Eben and Polly Dean; Orpha, Amos and Horatio Warner; Betsey and Hiram Hayden; Rhoda and Roman Agard; Sylvia Pease: George and David Miller; Lydia Blocker; Lucia, John and Edward Brown; and Levira Durham. The first school-house was built in the fall of 1816. The first school in that house was taught by Marcus Brown, (now Dr. Brown, of Circleville, Ohio.)

The first child born in the township was Alonzo Durham. Mrs. Dean and Mrs. Durham came on the 17th of March, 1814. From that time Mrs. Dean saw no woman but Mrs. Durham until the next August, and Mrs. Durham saw no woman but Mrs. Dean till October following. In the meantime, in July, Alonzo Durham was born. He resides in Indiana. The first person born, who resides here, is Eli Baron, son of Christopher Baron, born June, 1817. The first person that died in the township was Daniel Ware. He died in 1817, of fever. He was from Cumberland county, Pennsylvania.

The first persons married were George Baron and Margarett Smith, February 25th, 1814. The services were performed by Salmon Warner, Esq., one of the first Justices. The first religious meeting was at the house of Oliver Durham, in July, 1814. The services were conducted by Daniel Dean and Salmon Warner. The first sermon was preached in 1815, by the Rev. O. G. Gillmore, of the Methodist connection. The first church organized was the Methodist, in 1815. The members were Salmon Warner and wife, Oliver Durham and wife, Harriet Warner, Mrs. Kirkham and Mrs. Wright, in all seven. All are now dead but two.

The Congregational church was organized August 8th, 1819. The members were Frederick Brown and wife, Augustus Mills and wife, George Lyman and wife, Benjamin Agard, Sherman Loomis and Jacob Lindley, in all nine. Only two are still living, George Lyman and wife. Rev. Joseph Treat officiated at the organization.

The Baptist church was organized in 1824. Members, Elder Obediah Newcomb and wife, William Eyles and wife, Richard Clark and wife, Samuel Green and wife, and Mrs. Batison.

The first board of trustees consisted of Frederick Brown, Samuel M. Hayden and Jacob Miller. Justices of peace, Salmon Warner and Joseph Loomis. Constable, Reuben T. Warner. About forty voters. This was while the township was connected with Norton, and then called Wolf Creek township. At the first election after the township was detached from Wolf Creek, and organized by itself and called Wadsworth, held on the 6th day of April, 1818, were duly elected, Joseph Loomis and Salmon Warner, Justices of the Peace; Frederick Brown, Jacob Miller and Daniel Dean, Trustees; Samuel Blocker and Joseph Loomis, Overseers of the poor; Samuel M. Hayden, Lister; Lysander Hard, Treasurer; George Lyman and Wm. C. Richards, Constables; Sherman Loomis, Clerk; John Wilson and Jacob Miller, Fence Viewers.

George Lyman was constable two years in succession, and performed nearly or quite all the business of constable. His fees amounted to one dollar; and that for advertising and selling a stray horse.

The first law-suit in the township was between John Reed and Henry Falkner, before Esq. Warner. Falkner had bought a cake of tallow of Reed, and found, on examination, that it contained a piece of green beech wood, weighing about three pounds, upon which he refused to pay. Justice Warner decided that Reed should pay the cost and lose the tallow.

The first installed minister of the Congregational Church, was Rev. Amasa Jerome, in the fall of 1827. The Revs. Simeon Woodruff, Lathrop and Robins, officiated. The services were performed in Mr. Benj. Agard's frame barn, it being the most suitable place in the township.

The first physician in the place was Dr. John Smith; the second, Dr. Nathaniel Eastman.

While Dr. Smith was in practice, he had a patient, a young man, very sick with a fever. He was a single man and boarded at the house of Moody Weeks. Among the Dr's. prescriptions for the sick man, was a very large quantity of white coated pills, and these constituted the sum of the medicine. The unusual quantity the sick man was required to take, excited the curiosity of Mrs. Weeks to know what they were. On examination she found they consisted of unground black pepper rolled in flour. After Dr. Smith moved to the west part of the township, he was in the habit of sending his boy to A. & J. Pardee's store for whiskey. The following is an exact copy of twenty or more orders, all exactly alike.

"MESSRS. A. & J. PARDEE—
Gents: give the boy two jugs of whiskey, stop the jugs tight, help the boy on the horse.
JOHN SMITH, Physician."

Timothy Hudson built the first frame barn, in 1819. Benjamin Agard built the first frame house, in 1824. Joseph Loomis, Sherman Loomis, Abel Beach and George Beach built the first saw mill, in 1824. They had every thing ready to start their mill except a very little fixing, and left it on Saturday evening, in the month of January. During the night it rained considerably, and that with the melting of the snow, caused a freshet; os that the next morning the dam, mill and all, had gone down stream. They rebuilt again the next year. Allen and John Pardee built the first grist mill, in 1829. Benjamin Agard cleared the first land free from all the timber, in the spring of 1818. The universal method had been to clear off the small timber and girdle the large trees, and leave them standing. In April, 1817, there was not a tree cut on the center road, between the center of Wadsworth and Harrisville, and no settlement in Sharon, which was then a part of Wolf Creek township, but afterwards called Hart & Mather.

In the spring of 1824, the daughter of Abel Beach, aged twenty-six years, was lost. She left her father's house in the dusk of evening, April 17th. There was a squall of snow following a thunder shower, a little before she was found to be missing. There was a large chopping around the house, with the brush unburned.

This chopping and all the vicinity were searched through the night in vain. To call was of no use, as she was a deaf mute. In the morning her tracks in the snow were discovered leading in a straight line, in a south-west direction, but as the snow melted early in the morning, all trace of the poor girl was lost. At once, and for two or three days, the search became general, east west, north and south, but all in vain. The girl was never found, nor any sign or vestage or scrap of clothing, or remains whatever.

In 1811, flour was very scarce. Aaron Norton and another man had been south and obtained some flour for the army at Cleveland. They boated up the Tuscarawas to New Portage, then passed over by teams to Cuyahoga Portage. Application was made to Mr. Norton for some of the flour, by Mr. Dean; but Norton would not break a barrel or sell one for less than seventeen dollars. Mr. Dean had to go to Talmadge and procure a little, and in harvest go and work to pay for it. In 1814, flour was seventeen dollars per barrel, wheat three dollars per bushel, and salt twenty dollars per barrel, in Cleveland.

In early times we had some "mighty hunters" in Wadsworth. Among the most prominent were Orrin Loomis, Phineas Butler, David Blocker, Timothy Dascomb and William Simcox. Bears, deer, turkeys and coons were then plenty. Loomis and Butler killed the most bears and coons, and Blocker the most deer. Simcox was not far behind—he actually killed nine deer and one bear in a day.

Loomis had a dog that was famous for treeing bears and when once fairly treed, they might as well surrender and come down as to wait for Loomis to shoot, as he hardly ever failed of securing his prey. Judge Brown told me that in 1816, the settlers were in a great measure dependant on Loomis and his dog for meat through the summer. One thing the Judge remarked was a little peculiar—the old dog was altogether the most successful on the Sabbath; yet owing to the scarcity of provisions they did not deem it best to prosecute the dog.

There were likewise plenty of rattle-snakes. Geo. Lyman killed eight in one day; seven of them he found in a small hollow log, the eighth was by himself, and a very large one indeed.

WADSWORTH STATISTICS.

PERSONAL PROPERTY.	Number.	Value.
Horses,	669	$30,172
Cattle,	1,781	16,818
Sheep,	2,777	5,306
Hogs,	1,211	3,298
Merchandise,		6,472
Manufactures,		5,055
Carriages and Wagons,	403	10,897
Moneys and Credits,		41,160
Butter, pounds,	50,371	5,300
Cheese, "	3,200	190
Wheat, bushels,	26,255	26,255
Corn, "	68,590	17,145
Total value,		$168,171

If to the foregoing be added the value of all other products, the total will amount to two hundred thousand dollars.

WESTFIELD.

The township was originally owned by Samuel Fowler, of Westfield, Massachusetts, and Henry Thorndyke, Portage county, Ohio.

The first settlers were H. Palmer and Eben Mallory, in the spring of 1817. At that period there were settlements in Guilford and Harrisville, that more readily invited the speedy ingress of settlers into Westfield. Mr. Mallory and Mr. Palmer made the first opening on lot Ten, near the present residence of Mr. Daniels. Mr. Palmer still survives, residing with his son in Harrisville. Some of the family yet reside in the county.

Mr. Mallory came to his death in the following manner: while aiding his son in putting a saw-log on trucks, the chain that fastened the log broke and let it down upon him, causing instant death.

The first female child born in the township was Fanny Morton, in 1817. The first male child born was H. F. Mallory, in April 1818. The former resides in Lorain county, the latter in Illinois. The first person that died in the township was the wife of Alvah Beach, in August, 1821.

The first school was taught by Miss Hosmer, in the summer of 1818; and the first winter school was taught by Ansel Brainard, the following winter. The school house was eighty rods north from "Morse's Corners." The names of the scholars that attended school were Melissa, Theron and Alfred Harrington, Alonzo and Lewis Nye, Charles Mallory, Jane and Sherwood Palmer, Eliza, Lucy and Lorenzo Brainard.

The first marriage in the township was Mr. B. Flannigan to Miss Polly Cook, in June, 1819.

The Methodist Church was organized in 1819, by Ansel Brainard, Jr. The number and names of those then composing the organization are now forgotten.

In a few years thereafter the Baptist Church was organized; also the Congregational Church. Since the organization of these churches the accession in membership has been great and exerts a salutary influence in the township.

In 1820, the township was organized. At the first election twenty-six votes were polled. Messrs. Vaughn, Hamilton and Brainard were the first Trustees; and George Collier. Clerk. Rufus Vaughn was the first Justice of the Peace. For several years prior to the organization, Westfield was attached to Harrisville and listed as part of that township. After the first openings were made the township filled rapidly with settlers, and in 1821, Westfield was considered as "pretty well filled with settlers." The privations they encountered were somewhat similar to those were that endured in other sections of the county.

How striking the contrast between the appearance exhibited in 1818, and that seen in 1861. The forest is tamed, the wild beasts have fled, the visage of the red man is no longer visable; in their stead can be looked upon, with delight and gratitude, waving fields of grain in its season, heards of tamed cattle, and a dense population of orderly, industrious, moral, church going, patriotic citizens. The hastily constructed cabins are supplanted by commodious dwellings, the old log school house in which the first school rallied, has disappeared, and the township is dotted over with educational dwellings giving evidence of the improved state of society.

WESTFIELD.

Upon a portion of the forest where George Collier and others, forty-four years since, were accustomed to roam in search of wild game, can now be seen Churches, mechanic shops, and a dwelling owned by the Farmers' Insurance Company, that indicate the foresight and perseverance of the citizens. In every county in the State notoriety is given to the Insurance Company, and the safe way in which its financial operations are conducted, give assurance that it is a safe Company.

WESTFIELD STATISTICS.

PERSONAL PROPERTY.	Number.	Value.
Horses,	428	$20,280
Cattle,	1,473	15,670
Sheep,	7,133	12,135
Hogs,	922	2,564
Carriages and Wagons,	120	4,225
Moneys and Credits,		36,551
Butter, pounds,	52,285	5,230
Cheese, "	36,890	2,370
Wheat, bushels,	12,631	12,631
Corn, "	35,980	8,995
Total value,		$120,651

If to the above be added the avails that yearly result from the products of all other articles, the total will amount to one hundred and fifty-five thousand dollars.

YORK.

Although the township was not organized as early as 1826, yet a goodly portion (fourteen thousand one hundred and thirty seven acres) of the lands comprised within its present limits, were on duplicate for taxation. In that year Fanny Chapman, Elijah Hubbard, James Mather, Samuel Mather's heirs, Thomas Mather, Thomas Sill and William N. Sill, owned fourteen thousand one hundred and thirty-seven acres, valued at $29.936, on which a tax of $295,62 was paid. At that date there is no report of any personal property being listed and returned for taxation.

In 1830 George Wilson, of Monroe county, New York, settled in York township, made the first purchase and erected the first cabin in September, and may be called the first settler. In the next month (October, 1830,) Levi Branch, Lawson Branch, Rufus Stickney, Ezekiel Bruce, Solomon Hubbard, E. Munger and John Dunsha, removed from Sweden, in Monroe county, New York, and settled in the township.

The first election held in the township, was in the barn of Mr. Branch.

The first religious meeting ever held in the township was in the house of Mr. Branch. It continued at intervals, for seven weeks, and a marked change in actions was visible in all who attended those meetings.

Prior to the coming of the first settlers, they had been notified by letters that the Norwalk Road was located through the township, and was a good turnpike road; and that Mallet Creek abounded with speckled trout. Upon their arrival they found it necessary to make their own road, and as for trout they never found any of the speckled tribe but could daily see plenty of speckled frogs in the swampy lands without visiting Mallet Creek. Prior to the clearing of the level lands there were many swamps and pools of water.

The first child born in the township was Fanny Chapman Branch, daughter of Lawson and Cordelia Branch.

The first death and burial in the township was a son of John Dunsha. The first school was kept by Theodore Branch in one part of Levi Branch's dwelling. Rev. S. V. Barnes was the first preacher that addressed a congregation in the township. The place of congregating was for several years at the house of Levi Branch.

L. Branch owned the only team, and spent most of the first winter, after the arrival of the foregoing settlers, in making roads and traveling to Wooster, Portage and other places, to procure provisions. In the winter of that year a goodly number of settlers came in, and by the following spring there was quite a community.

April 2nd, 1832, the township was organized by electing Levi Branch, Thomas Brintnall and Sylvanus Thun, Trustees; Philo Fenn, Treasurer; and Alexander Forbs, Clerk. At that election twenty votes were cast, which was then thought to be rather a large election.

On 27th April, 1833, a Congregational Church was organized under the supervision of Revs. Barnes and Noyes, numbering twenty-six members.

In a few years thereafter a Methodist class was formed, a neat building erected, and now a respectable church established.

Alexander Forbs was elected Justice of the Peace in 1832, and during his legal term was hardly ever annoyed by litigants seeking legal redress for supposed grievances.

York township has, in twenty-nine years, thrown off every appearance of ever having been a fishing pond of "speckled trout," and become one of the prime townships in the county for grazing and agricultural purposes. Its rapid advances can be evidenced from examining the statistics here given for 1861.

YORK STATISTICS.

PERSONAL PROPERTY.	Number.	Value.
Horses,	444	$15,708
Cattle,	1,284	12,519
Sheep,	10,145	15,710
Hogs,	413	1,297
Carriages and Wagons,	141	2,752
Moneys and Credits,		68,478
Butter, pounds,	27,611	2,761
Cheese, "	8,090	500
Wheat, bushels,	5,897	5,897
Corn, "	22,145	5,516
Total value,		$131,136

If the sums that accrue from the yearly growth of all other articles, be added to the above, the total will amount to one hundred and sixty thousand dollars.

INDEX

----, Aaron 144 Jared 156-157 Jonathan 157-158 Justus 156 158 Lucinda 149 Nathan 157-158 Nep 1553 Oliver 145-146 148 Robinson 149 Ruth 147 Sally 149 Seba 156-159 Simon 158
ABBOTT, F A 177 188
ADAMS, 93 192
AGARD, Benj 215 Benjamin 214 216 Rhoda 213 Roman 213
AINSWORTH, 99
ALBERT, F A 182
ALLEN, David 186
ALLY, William 213
ANDROS, Thomas 199
ANGS, H 108
ARMSTRONG, Andrew 206
ASHLEY, Olivia 44
ATHERTON, G F 187 196 George F 198
ATKINS, Charles 122 Elizabeth 122

AUSTIN, Calvin 74 Eliphalet 87
BABBITT, Caroline 187
BABCOCK, D 107 David 107
BADGER, A 187 195 Austin 187 194 196 Catharine 187 Mr 198
BALDWIN, Geo J 44 George J 40 George W 36 Mary 70-71 Mr 71 Nancy 44
BALL, Jacob 62
BANGS, E 108
BARKER, 99 Chauncy 61-62
BARNES, Carlos 181 Dr 98 Eliza 184 George 181 Giles 184-185 187 Isaac 178 183-185 John 185 Lester 181 Lucius 181 Marther 185 Rev 223 S V 187 223
BARNS, Giles 185 John 185 Wm 96
BARON, Christopher 212-213 Eli 213 George 214 Margarett 214 William 212

BARRETT, Alexander 167
BARTHOLOMEW, Charles 32
BATISON, Mrs 214
BATTELL, Joseph 87 William 87
BEACH, Abel 216 Alvah 219 Dr 206 George 216
BEARD, Asa 122
BEAUMONT, Mr 106
BEERS, Mr 161
BELL, James A 62 John 62 66 206 Nathaneal 62 Nathaniel 63-64 W H 61 William H 60 Wm H 61
BELLAMY, Anson 167
BEN, Wm 79
BERDAN, A 35 John 35 Peter 35-36
BEZARD, Phillip 208 Ruth 208
BIGELOW, John 114 140
BIGLOW, Widow 75
BIRGE, David 96-97 Diadema 97 Mr 97
BISHOP, Elisha 96 William 208
BISSELL, Erastus 205
BISSETT, Elizabeth 208 Margaret 208 William 167
BIVENS, Lorenzo 204
BLAKESLEE, Burrit 190 Gad 189
BLAKSLEE, Chauncey 181 Gad 182 Mr 182
BLEAKS, 206 John 205
BLOCKER, David 217 Lydia

BLOCKER (cont)
213 Samuel 213 215
BLOOD, Seth 35
BOARDMAN, Elijah 171 Homer 171 Mr 171 176
BOGUE, Daniel 37 Henry 35 40
BOUGHTON, Guy 24
BRADFORD, Widow 179
BRAINARD, Ansel 219 Ansel Jr 220 Eliza 219 Lorenzo 219 Lucy 219 Mr 220
BRANCH, Cordelia 223 Fanny Chapman 223 L 223 Lawson 222-223 Levi 222-223 Mr 222 Theodore 223
BRAY, Rial 112
BRECK, Rev Mr 97
BRIGGS, John 186 Zepheniah 171
BRIGHAM, Eben 61
BRINTNALL, Thomas 223
BROMON, Mr 179
BRONSON, 195 Isaac 190 Levi 133 Louisa 131 Miss 132 Noah M 176 183 186
BROOKS, Abraham 167-168 Asenath 168 Fanny 168 Ira 168 Peter 168 Tabitha 168
BROWN, Dr 213 Edward 213 Frederick 213-215 John 213 Judge 217 Lucia 213 Marcus 213 Mr 23 109 Samuel 187 196
BRUCE, Ezekiel 222
BRUNSKELL, Joseph 206

BUCK, Dorman 106
BULLARD, Curtis 107-108
 Sarah 108
BURDICK, Hezekiah 75
BURGE, John 206
BURR, 91 Alpha 98 Geo 91 94
 George 89 97-98 101 Harris
 91 Hulda 98 Justus 95 98
 Mehetable 97-98 Mr 91-92
 Russel 87 97 99 Russell 89-
 91 95 Timothy 96-97 101
BURT, John 67
BUTLER, Phineas 217
CALENDER, Frank 181 Mr
 178 Philander 181
CAMPBELL, Elizabeth 122
CANFIELD, Judson 171
 William H 195
CARR, 108 Harriet 107-108
 John 108 Mr 107
CARTER, 174
CASE, Reuben 63
CASS, Nedabiah 54
CATLIN, Eunice 97 Isaac 96-
 97
CAUGHEY, 62
CHAMBERLIN, 174-175
CHAMPION, Aristarchus 187
CHAPIN, Seymour 35
CHAPMAN, 99 Arvis 96
 Cyrus 61 96 Fanny 222
 Jerusha 61 Leonard 98 101
 Levi 95 98 Perrin 101
 Perrine 98 Reuben 98
CHARLES, II King Of
 England 5 King Of ? 5

CHASE, Caleb 195
CHESTERFIELD, Lord 93
CHITTENDEN, Henry 93
CHURCHILL, Diadema 97
 Miss 97
CLARK, 142-144 B B 24 191-
 192 195 Bela B 182 John 183
 John L 182 P 35 R 195
 Ransom 182 184 Ricahrd 214
CLOSE, Deacon 109 Esquire
 55
CLUTE, David 64
CODDING, Burt 67 69 George
 M 68 John 67 69 Miss 204
COGSWELL, 105 Edward 72
 Mr 104 110 Nathaniel 75
 Samuel 72 75 W 71 William
 71-73 75
COIT, H 140 H H 134-135 Mr
 77 128
COLE, Ira 208 W 162 164
COLLIER, George 220-221
CONANT, Chester 106-107 D
 M 106-107
CONVERSE, William 164
CONYER, D 164
COOK, Apollos 167 Cyrus 161
 Polly 220 T B 167
CORBIN, 91 Calvin 89 Lyman
 89
COYT, Henry 113
CRANE, Barnabas 199 Bernice
 199 Jemimah 199 William
 199
CRANNY, Clarissa 133
CRAWFORD, James 60 62

CRAWFORD (cont)
  John 60-61 Josiah 62 Mr 94
  William 62
CRITTENDEN, Lydia 44
CROCKET, Davy 100
CROSBY, Samuel 68
CROSS, 95 Jesse 94 Samuel 94
  Theophilus 94
CROW, Mr 163
CURRIER, T M 196 Thomas
  195-196 Thomas M 187
CURTIS, Cyrus 96-97 Job 87
  Joel 40 Julia 108 Miss 108
DAKE, J B 109
DAMON, Caleb 109 Mrs 109
DANIELS, Barney 54 56 Mr
  219
DASCOMB, Timothy 217
DAVIS, Job 96 Phineas 208
DAY, Lucy 167
DAYKIN, Joseph 206
DEAN, Daniel 212 214-215
  Eben 213 Moses 213 Mr 212
  217 Mrs 213 Polly 213
DELVIN, Daniel 96
DEMING, Andrew 35 40 44
  Charles R 99 F 108-109 Fred
  107 Frederick 35 44 106 Mrs
  F 108 Roxanna 37 44
  Solomon 35 37 40
DEMMING, 148 160 Anna
  125 Clarissa 133 149 David
  128 Jerusha 134 John 125
  Moses 125 142 144 Mr 143
  Ruth 127 142-144
DICKESON, D W C 162

DOAN, 180 Jared 181 Jim 148
  Mary 181 Mr 34 132 174 T
  195 Thos 34 Timothy 34 174
  178 184
DOANE, Rozetta 168
DOANES, Isaiah 168
DOTHEE, Adaline 62
DOTY, Emelia 168 Jeremiah
  168 Susan 168
DUNBAR, John 202
DUNSHA, John 222-223
DURHAM, Alonzo 213 Levira
  213 Mrs 213 Oliver 212 214
DYER, Weathly 68
EASTMAN, Dr 64 Nathaniel
  215
EASTON, 106 T N 107
  Temperance 108 Thomas 108
  Thomas N 107 Thomas W
  108
EDWARDS, Harvey 54
EILCOX, Thomas 162
ELEY, Justin 59
ELY, William 212
EVERHARD, Christian 212
  John 212
EYLES, William 214
FALCONER, Margaret 208
  Samuel 208
FALKNER, Henry 215
FENN, Philo 223
FERRIS, Esq 23-24 177-178
  189 Mr 43 Mrs 176 R 195
  Rufus 42-43 176 178 184 T
  N 109
FINLEY, Lewis 162 164

FISK, J 106 Jonathan 107-108
    Mary 108
FITCH, Luther 205-206
FITTS, Jonathan 96
FLANNIGAN, B 220 Polly
    220
FLETCHER, Ephraim 37
FORBS, Alexander 223-224
    Emeline 62
FOWLER, J 169 S 167 169
    Samuel 219 T 167
FRANCIS, Darius 36 40
FRAZELL, Catharine 55
FREEMAN, Rufus 64
FREESE, Abram 36 B W 35
    John 35 45
FREEZE, A 106-107 109
    Abraham 105 107 John 191
FRENCH, Philo 60 213
GANYARD, Festus 67 71 J N
    70 James 67 69-71 John M
    68 Mr 69 Phebe 67 69-70
GARDNER, Gideon 56
GATES, Gideon 75 Lt 72
    Uncle 110 112-113
GAYLORD, Nehemiah 87
    Stewart 76
GIBBS, Horace 206 Milo 206
GILLETT, Jabes 87 John 87
GILLMORE, O G 214
GOLDEN, E 13
GOODELL, Joel 168
GOODWIN, Deborah 68 N A
    67 Phebe 208
GOUCH, Joseph 106
GRAHAM, Mrs 181

GRANGER, Gideon 69 Mr 69
GREEN, Asenath 204 Dexter
    204 Job 74-75 Lyman 203-
    204 Orpha 204 Samuel 214
    Seymour W 68 Stephen 202
GRIFFIN, James 68 Lomer
    101 Ralzmund 101 Samuel
    68 Somer 98 Willis 101
GROVER, Phebe 68
GUNN, Horace 34 Mr 34
HAINES, Joseph 87
HALE, E 79 Elijah 79
    Jonathan 79 Mr 79 83 Mrs
    79
HALL, Henry F 167 Nathan 97
    Pemilri 97
HALLADAY, Mr 163
HAMILTON, Arza 186 Eden
    186 Eden Jr 186 Elizabeth
    181 Esq 184 191 Joseph 181
    Lindley 186 Mary 181
    Matthew 181 Mr 172-173
    220 Ruth 181 Z 175 Zenas 7
    172 174 178 181 184 190
HANCHET, Amos 213 Heman
    213
HANFORD, Mr 185 W 67
    William 44 178 185
HANNA, Geo 96
HARD, Lysander 215
HARRINGTON, Alfred 219
    Benjamine 98 Hulda 98
    Melissa 219 Reuben 98
    Stephen 98 208 Theron 219
    Weava 98 Z 208
HARRIS, Albert 101 Ed 98

HARRIS (cont)
  Ephraim 167 Epraim 167
  Joseph 7 87-88 101 Judge
  101 Mr 23 88-94 96 Mrs 89
  93
HART, 202 204 216
HARVEY, Polly 44 Solomon
  35 40
HAYDEN, Betsey 213 Hiram
  213 Samuel 205 Samuel M
  213-215
HEADLEY, Capt 133
HEATHMAN, Esquire 99
HICKOX, 195 A G 192 Esq
  188 Harvey 178 John 178
HIGBEE, J 99
HIGH, William 206
HILL, Abigail 67
HILLARD, Gordon 213
HILLIARD, Diadema 97
  Gardon 97
HILLS, Abigail 67 Chester 204
  Eleazer 69 Elizar 67 Myron
  204 Tracy 204
HINCKLEY, 105 Judge 106
  Mrs R 141 Rhoda 151
  Samuel 104
HINMAN, J L 162 Mr 162 171
HOIT, Seth 187
HOLCOMB, Hannah 97 L 99
  Laura 98 Levi 98 Loammi
  96-97 101 Noah 96
HOLMES, David 68 204 Judge
  161 Mr 204
HOSMER, 66 Chester 59 61
  Henry 59-61 63-64 Jerusha

HOSMER (cont)
  61 Mary T 59 Miss 219
  William 60 63
HOWD, Albert 162 Asahel
  162-164 Caroline 162 E 163
  Eliphalet 162 Elizabeth 162
  Henry 162 James 162 John
  162 Judah 162
HRRRIS, Mr 93
HUBBARD, 144 Elijah 167
  222 Solomon 222
HUDSON, David 140 Henry
  68 83 Timothy 213 216
HULET, Hannah 44 John 35
  37 40 44 John Jr 40 Mr 175
HULETT, Mr 183
HULL, 91 147-148 Benjamin
  178 Benjamine 184 Elijah 40
HUMPHREVILLE, Eliza 182
  Mrs Judge 182
HUMPHREY, Luther 97
HUNTINGTON, Hezekiah 87
  Thomas 87
HUNTNGTON, Mr 129
HURLBERT, Mrs 44
INDIAN, King Phillip 182
INGERSOL, R 107
INGRAHAM, Friend 67 Ira 67
  Lydia 67
IRVIN, B 208
ISBEL, Lyman 82
ISBELL, Mr 83
IVES, Friend 190 Mr 190-191
  Mrs 190
JACKSON, 201
JACOBS, John 144

JEFFERSON, 192 200-201
JEROME, Amasa 215
JOLINE, Eleanor 55 Henry K 55-56
JONES, John 108 Myra 108
JOSLINE, Henry K 96
KELLOGG, Martin 87 Noah 96
KELLUM, Rev 168
KELSEY, Francis 76 Zenas 76
KING, Mrs Salmon 109
KINGSBURY, Jabez 37 44 Persis 37 44
KIRKHAM, Mrs 214
KNOW, Seymour 36
KNOWLES, Anna 125
LANE, John C 107
LATHROP, 215
LEFFINGWELL, Eveline 168 Matthew 168
LELAND, 62
LEWIS, Charles 96
LINDLEY, Eliada 33 Ephraim 32 36 40 Jacob 214
LONG, Dr 174
LOOMIS, 87 218 Alvia 96 Amasa 97 I 106 Jacob 108 Joab 107 Joseph 213-216 Lucy A 168 Milo 168 Orrin 217 Samantha 108 Sherman 214 216 Zilpah 108
LOON, Sherman 215
LOW, 69 Anthony 68-71 Hamilton 68 Hiram 68 Isaac 74 76 Mary 70-71 Mr 68
LOWERMAN, George 204

LOWERMAN (cont) Polly 204 Susan 204
LUCAS, Martha 168
LUCE, Erastus 175 195
LYMAN, George 212-215
LYON, Joel 54 56
M'CLOUD, Hannah 68
M'CREERY, Andrew 107
M;FARLEN, John 68
MADISON, 192 James 155
MALLET, Dan 78 John 149 Noah 149 Wilmot 149
MALLORY, Charles 219 Eben 219 H F 219 Mr 219
MANNING, John 75
MARSH, 174-175 Abijah 184 Asa 154 Clement 181 Freeman 181 Jacob 175 John P 208 Laura 98 Nathan 96 Samuel 208
MATHER, 202 216 James 222 Samuel 222 Thomas 222
MATHERS, 202 204
MAY, L 75
MCFARLIN, Almina 204 Almira 204 Charles 203-205 Esther 204 Irena 204 John 204 Melinda 202 Merina 204 Moses 204 Orville 204 Reuben 204 Wilson 204
MCGREGOR, John 206
MILES, Archibald 99
MILLER, David 213 George 213 Jacob 213-215
MILLS, Augustus 213-214 D 183

MOFFATT, Lemuel 167
  Samuel 167
MONROE, Nancy 187
MOODY, Ephraim 213 Ira 213
MOORE, 186 Amer 62 Jacob
  62 James 23 173 180 184
  James H 95 Lawrence 68
  Martha 204 Mary 68 Mr
  175-176 204-205 Peter A
  204-205 William 59 Wm 60
MORE, Mr 175
MORGAN, Mr 133
MORTON, Fanny 219
MOSES, Mr 164
MOTT, Ezekiel 68 Mr 175
MUDDIMAN, Mr 151
MUNGER, E 222
MUNSON, 174 Ebenezer 101
  Harmon 188 Herman 192
  Lyman 59 61 Mr 188-189
  Nancy 61 Timothy 96
NETTLETON, David 175 186
  Mrs 181
NEWBURY, Roger 59
NEWCOMB, Obediah 214
NICKERSON, Almira 164 O
  162
NOBLE, Moses 59
NORTH, Lemuel 213
NORTHROP, Charity 185
  Cornelius 108 Daniel 175
  Dathan 176 Eliza 181 184
  John 178 Joseph 43 176 184-
  185 Mary 108 Mr 184 N B 4
  177-178 190 Nathan 175
  Nira B 185 Noice B 176

NORTON, 93 Aaron 217 Mr
  217
NOYES, Rev 223
NUNN, Elder 68
NYE, Alonzo 219 Levi 62
  Lewis 219
OLCOTT, George 162-164
OVIATT, Erastus 108 Julia
  108
OWEN, Samuel 61
PACKARD, Amasa 54 56
  Amasa Jr 54 Catharine 55
  Celia 55 Cornelia 55 Emeline
  55 George 56 Iram 54 56
  Jacob 56 Philip 56 Polly 55
  Richards 55 Sarah 56
PAINTER, William 178 184
PALMER, Chloe 55 Eliza 55
  H 219 James 174-175 184
  Jane 219 Joseph 55 Liusa
  181 Lois 181 Lydia 55 Mr
  219 Sherwood 219 Thomas F
  54
PARDEE, A 216 Allen 216 J
  216 John 216
PARK, John 208 Mr 122
PARKER, Henry 35 40
PARKS, Harriet 122 James 122
  Mr 122
PARMALY, Asahel 182
PARSONS, Eleanor 55 Moses
  54 56 Samuel H 56
PAUL, S 67 Seth 67 William
  67-68
PAYNE, Mrs 34 Widow 34
PEASE, Sylvia 213

PELTON, Henry 187 Mr 163
  Parker 187 196
PERKINS, 94 Enoch 59 Gen
  93 Jesse 71 Josiah 96 100
  Simon 64
PERRY, 180 Capt 76-77
PHELPS, 75 Oliver 74
  Timothy 61
PHILLIPS, Agustus 182
PICKETT, D 162
PIMLOT, Joseph 187
PIPER, 106 Josiah 107 Mr 108
PITKINS, Caleb 67
POINT, Betsey 204 David 202-
  203 Jane 204 Marilla 204 Mr
  202-203 Mrs 202-203
POMEROY, G 164
POMROY, Rufus 68
POND, Henry N 188 Isaac J
  187 Mrs 188
PORTE, James 108
PORTER, 66 Abigail 60
  Abigal 59 Elijah 62 Ingersol
  106 Jehial 68 72 Mary 108
  Mr 62 Samuel 107 Shubal 59
  61-62
POTTER, Dr 148 S 195
  Samuel Y 178 184
PRATT, James 206
PRITCHARD, Capt 148
  Joseph 188 William 191
PUTMAN, 80
RANSOM, David 167 Henry C
  167
RAZOR, George 213
REDFIELD, James 101 James

REDFIELD (cont)
  S 88 96 99-101 Mr 100
REED, John 215
RICE, Anna 181 Capt 76
  Chloe 181 Cynthia 181
  Madison 181 Philemon 181
  Ruth 181
RICHARD, Jonathan 162
RICHARDS, Abigal 162
  Charles 162 165 Jonathan
  163 Julia 162 Verta 55
  William C 213 Wm C 215
RILEY, The Rover 104-105
  114
ROAD, Jacob 162
ROBERTS, Seth 176 189
ROBINS, 215 Brimel 76
ROCKWELL, Sol 87
ROGERS, David 96 Isaac 96
  James 96 98 101 Mr 98-99
  Nathaniel 96 Perez 96
ROOT, Frederick 36 G A 202
  Horace 36 40 W 35 Wm 36
RUDESILL, Jacob 202 205 Mr
  205
RUSSELL, Jerusha 134
  Thomas 96
SAINT, Clair Arthur 6
SALSBURY, Earl 85
SANFORD, Alva 187
SARGENT, Eliza 182
SAUSMAN, David 98
SAWYER, Widow 109
SCOFIELD, Mrs 132
SCOTT, Abraham 183-184
SCOVILL, 148

SCOVILLE, 143-144 148
  David 141
SEARL, Mr 178 181 Royce
  177 184
SEARLE, Mr 189 R 192
SEARS, Elisha 90
SEATON, Andrew 175 Mr 175
SEELEY, 143-146 Ely L 141
SELKIRK, H 190 Mr 191
SEVA, Levi 101
SEYMOOR, Mr 85
SEYMOUR, 69 Banner 181
  Capt 174 180 Harrison 181 L
  195 Lathrop 148 178-180
  Lothrop 114 184 Miles 178
  Mr 68 85 179 Mrs 179-180
SHALER, Israel 108 Mr 164
SHAW, Alfred 55 Ebenezer 54
  Ebenzer 56 Mary 55 Moses
  60 62 Mr 54 Orin 54-56
SHEAR, A 109
SHELDON, David 82 H O 208
SHEPHARD, 174
SIBLEY, E H 87
SILL, Thomas 222 William N
  222 Wm N 167
SIMCOX, Benjamin 213
  William 217
SIPPY, 80-82 84 I 79
SIZA, 99
SKINNER, Harriet 204 Roger
  171
SLATER, Ezekiel 167
SMITH, 212 A 196 Aaron 187
  196 Adam 213 Allen 68
  Amassa 187 Dr 215-216

SMITH (cont)
  Horace 187 Jacob 213 Jesse
  59 Jesse H 68 John 61 215-
  216 Jonathan 205 Margarett
  214 Mark 205 Rabecca 204
SOOY, Samuel 208
SPACE, Elizabeth 208 John
  208
SPENCER, Aaron 85
  Alexander 68 Bela 68 C R 74
  80 Jason 96 Lydia 68
SPOONER, Mr 145
STAFFORD, Z 162
STANLY, Titus 100
STARR, Edward 167
STEARN, James 35 John 35
STEARNS, C 36 Clarissa 44
  Daniel 36 40 James 36 40
  John 37-38 40 42 44 Lucy 37
  44 Lydia 37 44 Mr 42 Phebe
  44 Thomas 40 44 W P 37
  William P 44
STEBBINS, Harvey 35-36 40
STEVENS, Hiram C 155 W P
  35
STEVENSON, 186
STICKNEY, Rufus 222
STILES, Jonas 60-61
STILLMAN, Mr 106
STODART, Orange 96
STOW, 106 Thomas 107
STOWE, Capt 76 Rhoda 35
  43-44
STRAIT, Asa 162 164 J V 165
  Jane T 162 Mrs S 165 N 165
STRONG, Gov 104 Mr 173

STRONG (cont)
174
SULLIVAN, Lot B 187
SUTLIFF, 87
SWIFT, Richard 107 Richard Jr 109
TANNER, Mr 122
TAPPAN, Benj 6 John 212
TAYLOR, Cyrus 205
TERRILL, Oliver 144 148
THAYER, B 108 Jacob 108 Jared 106-107 L 35
THORNDYKE, Henry 219
THORNINGTON, Billy 92
THUN, Sylvanus 223
TILLOTSON, Samuel 35 37 44 Sarah 37 44
TODD, George 23 189 Judge 188
TOWNSEND, 155 Mrs 154
TRACY, Mordica 98
TREAT, Joseph 214
TRUMAN, John 85
TURNER, Charity 68 Dolly 67-68 Hannah 68 John 67 71
TUTTLE, Carolus 96-97 101
TYLEE, Royal 87
USHER, N L 106
UTTER, Amos 54
VALLAND, Abram 203 Polly 204 Rhoda 204 Sally 204 William 204
VANDVENTER, J 163
VANHEINANS, Esq 99
VAUGHN, George 203 Mr 220

WADSWORTH, Elijah 212 Gen 91
WAITE, Deacon 109
WALCOTT, William 60
WALLACE, George 168 Harriet 107
WALTMAN, Achsah 204 Valentine 204
WALTON, 105
WARD, Elizabeth 37 Isaac 36 Jacob 35-36 40 43 John 37
WARDEN, Mr 128
WARE, Daniel 213-214
WARNER, 160 Aaron 145-147 149 Adna 145-146 149 Alpheus 128 141 143-144 147-149 Amos 213 Daniel 212 David 178 E A 182 Esq 98-99 215 Father 128 130-132 Gaylord C 54 George 178 Grandpa 146-147 149-150 152 Harriet 213-214 Horatio 213 James 182 186 Jeremiah 191 Johnson 188 Jonanna 145 Justice 215 Justus 7 41 137 140-143 145 148-149 151 155 Justus Jr 145 Minerva 141 143-144 147-151 154 Mr 77 98 128 138-139 Mrs 136-137 Noah 176 Orpha 213 R F 212 Reuben T 214 Ruth 126-127 142 Sally 130 Sally Urania 143 Salmon 212 214-215 Urania 145 William 41 136
WASHINGTON, George 192

WEEKS, Moody 215 Mrs 215
WELCH, William 96
WELTON, Jacob R 186 Mirah B 178 Mr 23 198 Philo 187 Selden B 186
WETHERBY, 149
WHEELER, Hiram 108 Julia 108 Mr 163
WHITE, Elijah 59 George W 204
WILCOX, Abigal 162 George 162 Lucretia 162 O 104 Thomas 163
WILLEY, D 79 Joseph 202 Melinda 202
WILLIAMS, Duncan 123 Nancy 187 Roswell 168 W R 187
WILMOT, 160
WILSON, 66 Daniel 62 David 59-60 63-64 George 222

WILSON (cont) Harriet 63 James 204 John 59 61 63-64 215 Julia 106 Margaret 63 Mr 62 Nathan 106 Robert 63
WING, Mr 122
WOLCOTT, William 60-61
WOLF, 149
WOOD, Abel 208 Henry 208 Vivalda 167
WOODBRIDGE, Lydia 44
WOODROUGH, Simeon 139
WOODRUFF, S P 109 Simeon 44 108 185 215
WOODWARD, Abigail 67 John 206 Mr 184 Stephen 67 Wm 206
WORDEN, Roxy 151
WRIGHT, 87 Henry C 212 Mrs 214
YOUNG, Collins 96

www.ingramcontent.com/pod-product-compliance
Lightning Source LLC
Chambersburg PA
CBHW071434150426
43191CB00008B/1122